About the Author

Maria C. McCarthy was born in 1959 and raised in a community of Irish migrants in Epsom, Surrey. Her Irish heritage features strongly in her writing. She is the author of two poetry collections: *strange fruits* and *There are Boats on the Orchard*; a collection of linked short stories, *As Long as it Takes*; and is contributing editor of *Unexplored Territory*. All four books are published by Cultured Llama. She is also a contributing editor of *Inspired by Six Women Who Shook the World* (Medway Libraries). Maria was the winner of the Society of Authors' Tom-Gallon Trust Award 2015 for her short story *More Katharine than Audrey*. In 2011, she co-founded Cultured Llama Publishing with her husband, Bob Carling, and was poetry and fiction editor until the press closed in 2023. She has an MA with distinction in Creative Writing from the University of Kent. She lives in the Medway Towns.
www.medwaymaria.co.uk

Also by Maria C. McCarthy

strange fruits (Cultured Llama and Word Aid, 2011)

Unexplored Territory (Cultured Llama, 2012)

As Long as it Takes (Cultured Llama, 2014)

There are Boats on the Orchard (Cultured Llama, 2017)

Inspired by Six Women Who Shook the World, contributing editor with S.M. Jenkin (Medway Libraries, 2023)

Reviews

As Long as it Takes

A mirror, a christening gown, a comb, a child's tea-set or a set of Russian dolls: these things can be enough to set off a whole story. In fact, *As Long as it Takes* is a bit like a nest of Russian dolls, with one woman packed inside another woman, each helping to contain or release or the other.

Pauline Masurel, on *The Short Review*

Dark, impeccably minimalistic stories about immigrant Irish mothers and their English-born daughters … transcending painful differences with their courageous humour and absolute refusal to look away. The stories reinforce each and create memorable echoes, reverberating in the mind long after the book is closed.

Martina Evans, author of *The Coming Thing* (Carcanet Press)

McCarthy shares with William Trevor a profound melancholy and her tales, like the Irish landscape eternally showered with soft yet invasive rain, are similarly saturated in shame, sacrifice, and secret sorrow.

William Skinner, on *Writers' Hub*

There are Boats on the Orchard

This collection is a moving depiction of the changing face of our orchards, beautifully observed by a writer who cares deeply for the preservation of our natural world.

Neil Leadbeater, on *Write Out Loud*

strange fruits

…humane poems, which are both natural and skilful, and combine the earthiness and mysteriousness of life.

Moniza Alvi, author of *Fairoz* (Bloodaxe Books)

**For my beloved daughters, my granddaughter, my
husband, Bob, and for my chosen family**

In memory of

Lt Gen Jim Parker, 1929–2020, childhood friend of my
father, and much later my friend, penfriend, confidant,
and teller of terrible jokes

Karan Bucknall (née Regan), 1959–2020, second-generation Irish sister

John McCarthy, 1955–2022, my big brother, with love
from Cookie

Learning
to be
Irish

Learning to be Irish showcases the best new and collected writings of a child of Irish migrants. Raised in Surrey in the 1960s and '70s, 'the filling in the sandwich' of a family of five children, Maria C. McCarthy dances to Irish showbands, learns rebel songs at an uncle's knee, hears home truths, half-truths and white lies from the women that gather in her mother's kitchen, and learns to be English after the IRA bombs two pubs in Guildford. *Learning to be Irish* is a search for identity, a chronicle of a lost generation, and a yearning for truths that may never be known.

"**Maria C. McCarthy's** *Learning To Be Irish,* comprising poems, stories, and memoir, is a welcome addition to a wave of second-generation Irish writers born in England. McCarthy is a particularly fine poet, and I recommend her sequence 'Mitchelstown' to all who are interested in the delicate relations between native and exile. *Learning To Be Irish* can take its place alongside the work of such writers as Ian Duhig, Shane MacGowan, and Martina Evans. A terrific book."

John O'Donoghue, author of
Sectioned: A Life Interrupted,
The King From Over The Water and
The Servants and Other Strange Stories

"Quietly devastating. A mature and truthful exploration of complex emotions, conflicting loyalties, identity, belonging. Through her mastery of different forms of writing: poetry, story, memoir, McCarthy shows us the beating heart of the second-generation Irish in England."

S.M. Jenkin, author of
Fire in the Head and *Unspeakable,* and co-editor of
Inspired by Six Women who Shook the World

Learning
to be
Irish

Maria C. McCarthy

First published in May 2025

Siglum Publishing
Edinburgh
Scotland
www.siglumpublishing.co.uk

Production and design: Bob Carling www.carling.org.uk
Front cover picture: Maggie Drury
Cover design: Mark Holihan
Author Photo: Michi Masumi www.michimasumi.co.uk

ISBN: 978-1-9161733-4-7

A Catalogue record for this book is available from the British Library

So many years I've held the memory
of sailing to Dun Laoghaire
with my mother,
left with the luggage
while she searched for something lost.

From 'The Road to Mitchelstown'

Publisher's Preface

It is a particular delight and honour to add this fine volume of collected and new writings to Siglum's growing list. Maria C. McCarthy is an award-winning author and poet whose widely published work explores issues of personal and communal identity with insight, humour, subtlety… and some great stories!

As you will discover, *Learning to be Irish* is a deeply human book, and one which beautifully combines narrative, poems and memoire to shed light on what it means to live, breathe and have our being across different cultures, generations and experiences.

Herein lie many different joys, sorrows and questions – including tales of the unexpected which will intrigue, delight, surprise, arrest and provoke thought in the reader.

Our aim as a publisher is to share the work of high quality authors who use their art and craft not only to entertain, but also to help us to understand the world we share better and to appreciate it in an enriched way from different viewpoints. This book fulfils all of that promise, and more.

Simon Barrow
Director
Siglum Publishing

Contents

Story

I know this story:

it's one of nuns and Christian brothers;
    of drawing water from a well; of winters
        without shoes; of delivering your sister

when the midwife couldn't come; of finding
    a man in the barn, hanging; of sailing
        on the open deck of the night boat

to Holyhead with one suitcase, bearing
    two of everything; of working in a hospital; of sending
        money home; of cinemas and dancehalls and clinging

to your own; of meeting my father
    at a dance above the Gas Showrooms;
        of the pale blue wedding dress (five months gone);

of leaving the reception while he stayed on,
    drinking; of living with his mother
        who complained about a mark on the wall

made by the touch of the baby's fingers;
    of moving to a hostel whilst waiting to be housed
        (no men allowed); of travelling to Ireland

with my brother; of the farmer
    who would've taken you on, mother and son;
        of the older man in England, who courted

you before you met my father, who treated
    you to a show, Chu Chin Chow on ice,
        who walked his dog past our house

every day until he died, the house the council gave
   you once you had five, where my father
      led you a hell of a life with the drink

and the babies and the miscarriage;
   of the doctor who treated you like
      you'd brought it on yourself; of hiding

from the rent man; of us all turned out nice,
   hair brushed, clean socks, so the neighbours
      wouldn't know; of how you did it for us,

stayed with a man
   who was only home
      when the pubs closed,

or the horses ran
   the wrong way.
      I know this story;

it's yours, not mine. I've stopped listening.

Learning to be English

My parents met at a dance above the Gas Showrooms in Epsom in the mid-1950s. My father had come over to England from Mitchelstown, a small town in County Cork, in 1944; my mother from Ennistymon in County Clare in the early '50s. They married at St Clement's Roman Catholic Church in Ewell, my mother in a blue suit, five months gone, after falling pregnant with my brother John the first time she'd gone 'all the way' with my father on an autumn day on Epsom Common. She had the flu on their wedding day, and retreated from the reception early. Dad stayed on, drinking. He started as he meant to go on.

Mum and Dad stuck to their wedding vows until Death did them part forty five years on, despite not appearing to like each other, and went on to have four more children. I am in the middle, the filling in the sandwich, a sister and brother above me, a sister and brother below.

Aged roughly two years apart, all five of us went to St Joseph's RC Primary School. The school was a United Nations of Spanish, Italian, Polish and Irish children, the progeny of economic migrants, come to work in the seven hospitals that Epsom boasted at the time. These were the days when the people of London sent their troublesome relatives to the country, to asylums. Those with severe psychiatric illnesses (or 'milk fever', or other temporary disturbances that may have got better if they hadn't remained locked away for the rest of their lives), and those with what we then called mental handicap. My mother worked in West Park Hospital, which we called a 'mental hospital' back then, as a Nursing Assistant, and many of my friends' parents also had jobs in the hospitals.

My dad worked 'on the buildings', leaving in Uncle Bill's van before the rest of the house had risen, labouring on sites as long as there was daylight. Long days in the summer months, sometimes returning home for dinner long after the rest of the family had eaten, his plate kept warm on top of a saucepan of hot water, an upturned plate over the meal, so it looked like a flying saucer. If he had money, he'd go to The White Horse with Uncle Bill and the other men he worked with, and come home long after the gravy had congealed on the plate, the meat shrivelled, the potatoes and vegetables dried up.

We lived in a house allocated by the council after the prefab where I was born was deemed overcrowded. I was four when we arrived at the new house, the youngest of us a few months old, and that's where my parents lived out the rest of their lives, my brother John also ending his days there nearly 60 years after we all moved in.

The small estate of post-war houses, pebble-dashed and painted white, all with the same front doors and windows, nestled in an outer circle with small roads branching in and out. There were few car owners and little traffic, and games of Red Rover, British Bulldog and 'Please Mister Crocodile, may we cross your golden river in your golden boat?' took place on the street, but not on the one green on the estate where the man lived who punctured footballs that fell into his garden.

We lived amongst Sullivans, Corrigans, Regans and McLoughlins. We socialised with other Irish families at dances, weddings and parties. Coaches took us to the Irish dances at Surbiton Assembly Rooms, the women in long dresses, the men in suits, the girls in fancy dresses with new white socks, which would be black on the soles by the end of the night from sliding across the polished floor in the lobby. The women would gather with handbags on the tables, the ash growing on cigarette ends as they talked. The men stood at the bar, bringing Cinzano and lemonade for the women, Pepsi in glass bottles with straws for the children.

Although many men joined in the set dances, to the

music of an Irish showband, Dad and Uncle Bill were not amongst them, but Mum and her sister, Auntie Chris, were never short of partners. We children joined in, too, swept off our feet in the reels, dizzy as we were dropped back to the floor. I don't remember getting home. I must have been lifted, asleep, onto the coach and carried from the end of the road to our house, undressed and put to bed without waking.

There were parties at home, too. My mother was the eldest of fourteen, and quite apart from the brothers that came over from Ireland and stayed while they found work and somewhere to live, there were uncles in Acton, Auntie Chris who lived near to us, and Auntie Bridget in Orpington. The Acton and Orpington contingents would arrive unannounced, with none of the families being on the phone, armed with loaves of bread, joints of meat and bags of potatoes and vegetables. Auntie Bridget bring-ing not only her six children, but anyone else on her road that might want to tag along, plus her husband Matt and his brother who wore a hat with a small feather in it, and whom we knew only as Fairy. Uncle Matt had a bald patch, until one day he hadn't. He arrived one Sunday sporting an ill-matched toupee, and was thereafter referred to as Uncle Matt-on-his-head.

Sometimes the gatherings were Sunday lunchtime to early evening; other times the visitors would come on a Saturday and party into the night, with Irish records on the Dansette, singing and dancing. People would sleep wherever they found a space, only Chris and Bill returning home in the small hours. When Uncle Martin came from Acton, he would teach me Irish rebel songs as I sat on his knee, singing a line as he bounced me up and down, get-ting me to sing it back until the whole song stuck. 'Now, don't be singing those songs at school, or to your English friends,' he told me. He was the only one of the uncles who didn't drink alcohol, so he didn't join the men at the White

Horse for the Sunday lunchtime session. He and Auntie Marie didn't have children, and Martin loved giving us treats. My parents didn't drive; Martin drove a lorry for a living and owned a Mini. 'Who wants to go for a spin?' he'd ask, and as many of us as would fit piled into the car. He'd take us up to Epsom Downs, and try to scare us by taking his hands off the steering wheel for a few seconds. As we got older, if a work trip took him close to Epsom, he'd park the lorry outside our house and take a couple of us with him. Sitting high in the cab above the traffic, he'd put me in charge of navigating, a map laid across my lap. There would be stops at greasy spoon cafés for strong tea, toast and jam. Then we'd arrive at the drop-off and stay in the cab while the lorry was unloaded.

I could read before I started school, my big sister teaching me what she had been taught. It wasn't a household where we were read to by parents. There was no such thing as a bedtime story, except for those we girls made up and told each other in bed at night: the tale of the laughing machine gun and the crying revolver; the one about the witch who had a lift that went sideways as well as up and down; and imagining that there was a secret door from our room into the McLoughlins' house next door, so we could play with their children at night. My little sister was fond of telling us things that had happened to her when she was older, which often involved meeting an angel on the garden path as she was hanging out the washing, or having a son called Jonathan.

We were not cuddled or kissed as children. The only physical contact was a brisk rub down with a towel after a bath on Sunday night, an impatient combing through of tangles in the girls' long wet hair, a fierce brushing to raise it into a ponytail for school the next morning. Baths were shared, or if I had the privilege of a solo soak, it would be in the water that another had bathed in, grey with the dregs of soap and shampoo. An even greater privilege was having the first bath. I loved it really hot, so I could hardly bear to step into it and my skin turned scarlet. All that stopped once Pauline across the road fell into a bath as it was filling and ended up in hospital with burns. Cold water first became the rule.

Falls and cuts were greeted with tutting, a far from gentle cleansing of the wound, and applying a plaster, accompanied by Mum chanting, 'Oh, you'll die.' There was a pot of black goo kept in a kitchen cupboard, once given on prescription to someone in the family, kept for years afterwards, marked 'The ointment'. It was applied to every injury.

Every Thursday evening, Dad took coins and notes from a small brown envelope with his name written on it, and handed them to Mum for the housekeeping. She kept the coins for feeding the electric meter in the cupboard under the stairs. 'Money for the light,' she called it, shillings before decimalisation, fifty pence pieces after. Thursday was also the night we children were given our pocket money, and Kitty Sullivan came round to collect the Football Pools coupon. Columns were marked with Xs against the names of football teams in an attempt to predict the number of score draws the coming Saturday and win the jackpot.

Mrs Sullivan was always invited to sit for a while, interrupting *Top of the Pops* on the television, which she glanced at with disdain. She took in everything and everyone in the room, whilst sitting straight-backed on a dining chair. Mum used to say, 'If you met her at one end of the market, she'd have you undressed by the other end.' We all, including Mum, found her hard to converse with, sharing nothing in common apart from being Irish.

One Thursday night, she was sitting with her hands on her lap as usual, when Dad came in the room, and we gathered round him to claim our weekly payment. Kitty

Sullivan pursed her lips, and as we clamoured for our coins, she pronounced, 'In my young day, I didn't know what pocket money was.' The room went silent for a moment, we children tight-lipped, trying not to laugh. Once Mrs Sullivan had gone, we repeated her pronouncement, taking off her accent and demeanour. Mum tried to chastise us for being rude about our elder, but she too could not help but laugh. For many years after, whenever Mrs Sullivan's name was mentioned, it was always followed by: 'In my young day, I didn't know what pocket money was.'

Neither parent was confident about writing, and the only paper in the house was Basildon Bond, small pads of plain pages, with a lined sheet that could be placed beneath to keep the writing straight. This was only kept for important letters, like notes to school, which Mum asked me to write, and she would then sign. Basildon Bond was not for children, so I tore pages from the endpapers of Mum's books – Agatha Christie murder mysteries and Harold Robbins potboilers, stacked in a tea chest in the cupboard under the stairs – and I wrote with stubs of pens that Dad brought home from the bookies.

I used my pocket money to buy pens, pencils, rubbers, and red Silvine notebooks with weights and measures tables printed on the back. The covers were ridged and shiny, and I liked to trace my fingers over the whorled patterns. On the lined pages within, I wrote and doodled and drew pictures, all of which were only seen by me.

There were plenty of opportunities to write at St Joseph's: poems, stories, and 'What I did at the weekend,' a Monday ritual after the class had been quizzed on what colour robes the priest had worn at Sunday Mass, to check that we'd all been to church. I would report on the Old Mother Riley films and cartoons at Saturday morning pictures, a Beatles film if we were lucky, *Help* or *A Hard Day's Night*. I spent half a sixpence on a ticket to get in, and the other half on a 3D ice lolly or an Everlasting Toffee Strip.

The Odeon was packed with children, the only grown-ups being the ushers, a live band called The Squirrels, and the manager who would regularly stop the film and stand in front of the screen, shouting that it wouldn't recommence until the foot-stamping and shouting had stopped. I wasn't one of those shouting, stamping children. I was happy to lose myself in the goings-on on the screen, on a sugar high from my Saturday treats. Once, though, I was in the seat behind Terry Blackman, a boy from school whose hair stood on end, and who wore his school clothes at weekends. He was one of the foot-stampers, for sure. 'Do you know what sexy means?' he said, a slow grin spreading across his face.

'It means fat or thin legs,' I said, my knowledge gained from an overheard conversation at a neighbour's Christmas party, when Uncle Dave across-the-road told Auntie Pam across-the-road that she had sexy legs.

He laughed. 'Do you know what shag means?'

'It's to do with hair,' I said. He doubled over, sniggering. I thought I'd got it wrong, so I made another attempt. 'Is it to do with dogs?'

'Yeah, dogs do it,' he said, and then it went dark and the film began.

As the years went on, I became the one in charge, the older children in the family having moved on to spending time with friends at their new schools. Going to the pictures meant trailing a retinue of younger children; not just my own siblings, but any of their friends that wanted to tag along. It was the same for trips to the swimming baths with rolled towels clamped under the armpits and trips to The Chocolate Box afterwards. I was responsible for the walk to and from town, and the other children's behaviour at the Odeon or at Epsom Baths. Not so when I went to the library; my only solo venture of the week.

The others were not as excited as I was about exchanging cardboard tickets for up to three books, to be returned in two weeks' time. Neither were they interested in my retelling of the stories within the books' covers, something I also found with my classmates who were not as excited as I was about *Stig of the Dump* or *The Family from One End Street*.

I couldn't have been more than eight years old when I started my solo library adventures. They involved a walk into town, crossing busy roads, armed only with the safety of my library tickets. Amongst the many library books that I took home each week, there was one called *Gumphlumph* by Stratford Johns, which I chose because I recognised the author's name from the credits of *Z Cars*. With the telly the focus of the home, an actor's or celebrity's name would have been more familiar to me than that of any author.

I knew of Dickens through a dark-blue cloth-covered hardback, which held two books between its covers: *A Tale of Two Cities* and *A Christmas Carol*. My father had brought it home from a building site that he was working on, from a derelict room full of books that were being thrown away. I never tackled *A Tale of Two Cities*, but read and re-read *A Christmas Carol* as a child, and have loved the story ever since.

***

The packing for the annual trip to Ireland begins the night before: a pair of shoes for Christy, a bread knife for Gus, as Mum noticed his wasn't up to scratch when we went to Ennistymon last summer. 'Don't they have shoe shops in Ireland?' My question goes unanswered, so there is no point asking whether Irish shops sell bread knives. Mum is in a flurry of ironing clothes that she'll iron again when the suitcases are emptied when we arrive. There are new knickers and socks, as there are for each summer trip, one set to be worn on the journey. Good and favourite clothes have been washed, and we're not allowed to wear them the week before we set off for Euston to catch the train for Holyhead for the night crossing on the Hibernia to Dun Laoghaire.

Mum is scared of crossing London on the tube or the bus. I often wonder how she made it to Epsom when she first arrived from Ennistymon; having made the journey once, alone, she never wanted to try it again. So John Conlon drives us to Euston, leaving us in the car park below the station. From there, it's a long train journey, full of excitement and sandwiches until we fall asleep, only to be woken in the early hours as the train arrives at Holyhead. Sleep-walking children on a never-ending trek through the customs hall – where the bread knife goes through unchecked, a cross marked in white chalk on each suitcase.

We gather on the open deck around the luggage, surrounded by huddles of women and children, no men, as the dads have to stay home and work. A lady on her own starts chatting to Mum, and she stays with us when Mum goes to the tea bar or to the toilets. I fall asleep, and wake up later with my head on the lady's lap.

It feels like I'm still on the ship for ages after getting off. We get a train as far as Limerick, and onwards in Cyril Hynes's taxi to Ennistymon. The bed is floating, floorboards beneath are waves, rising and falling, in the room I share with Great Aunt Maura who wears holy medals in the pocket of her nightdress. They clink together when she turns in the night. She calls them, 'My little bit of religion.' Although she's holy, she swears a lot. When we arrived, it was raining, and she said, 'Jesus, lads, you brought the fecking weather with you.'

Since Nanny died, Grandad and Uncle Christy live together in a house up the Pound Road. Chickens wander in and out of the kitchen where Christy butters thick slices of bread and leaves a jam pot on the table. 'Work away,' he says, which means we can help ourselves. Christy wears wellies most of the time, but changes into shoes and clean clothes when Mum's around, as she's the big sister and in charge of all the aunties and uncles now Nanny is gone.

I can only remember meeting Nanny twice, once on a visit 'home', and once when she came to stay with us in Epsom. She looked like a Nanny from a story book, with round glasses and silver-grey hair tied in a bun at the back of her head. At night, her hair hung loose around her shoulders. It was my job to bring her a cup of tea in bed in the morning, and read to her from the *Daily Mirror* that Dad had brought home the day before. Mum didn't seem that pleased that Nanny was staying. I heard Dad say that there was 'no love lost' between my mum and her mum.

When Nanny died, Mum said she couldn't go to the funeral, with all of us to look after. We had to have the curtains closed and no television for a day. Mum looked angry rather than sad. She didn't cry.

Mum is like the Queen when she's 'home' in Ireland. She wears her best shoes and clothes, everyone knows who she is, and wants her to come round for tea and cake. We have to visit loads of people, as if she leaves anyone out they'll be offended, so we go from house to house and listen to all the old stories that we heard last year and the year before that. I like going to May Nestor's, who lives on a farm and has a fireplace so big that you can sit inside it. When we're not in people's houses, we can do what we like.

We go to the seaside at Lahinch, a couple of miles away. There is a tiny funfair, a cinema, a dance hall, and a café that advertises 'ices and minerals'. Minerals means fizzy drinks like red lemonade, which you can only get in Ireland. There is a sandy beach and it's very windy a lot of the time.

The cattle mart comes to Ennistymon on a Friday, and we perch on the top bars of the metal barriers and watch the cows and the farmers with Uncle Christy. Christy has a new donkey, and he lets me name it. I call it Bonnie.

Grandad hitches the donkey to a cart, and he rides to

Lahinch with his accordion to play in the pubs for the tourists. I'm a bit scared of Grandad. He has false teeth, and he lets the top set fall from his gums as a joke, but it's not funny. He mumbles in a voice I don't always understand. He likes hunting rabbits and talking along to the telly, saying everything that's going on in the programmes. At twelve o'clock and six o'clock there's the Angelus and you're supposed to stop and pray.

We go to St Michael's on a Sunday. The priest talks really fast, and Mass is over a lot quicker than at St Joseph's in Epsom.

Mum is really happy when she's at 'home'. She doesn't have bad moods, and she lets us stay up late. I cry when it's time to leave. I like it in Ireland. Grandad stands at his gate and says, 'I'll be dead the next time you come.' He says it every year. There's the long journey in reverse, to Limerick, to Dun Laoghaire, to Holyhead, to Euston, and then home in John Conlon's car. The waves of the ship last until I'll back in my own bed, the first night home, and then it's back to normal.

***

I was one of a handful of children from my class to pass the eleven-plus, and only the second child on our council estate to go to grammar school. I moved from the rough and tumble of St Joseph's to Rosebery County Grammar School for Girls. The back entrance to the school stood some fifty yards from our front door. I walked in every day through the tradesmen's entrance.

There were new hymns to learn from the *Songs of Praise* hymnbook with the light blue cover. All girls were required to own a copy, and though it took several weeks of term for my mother to buy one, reminded every time a teacher scolded me for being without the book, I quickly learned the songs by heart. The prayers at assembly were different from the Catholic ones I knew. 'For thine is the kingdom, the power and the glory' was an addition to the 'Our Father', which I learned was actually called 'The Lord's Prayer'. We'd never spoken those words at St Joseph's, which led me to believe that the non-Catholic God was different from the RC version.

There had been warnings at St Joseph's about my faith, if I were to go to a non-Catholic secondary school. Mr O'Callaghan, my teacher in the Top Class, had urged my mother to send me to St Andrew's, not only because of the threat of a non-Catholic environment, but as she related to me from their conversation: 'The cream of the best brains is going to the grammar school,' and as I would do well in any school, I should go to a Catholic one. A mother's pride prevailed, and to the grammar I would go.

It had been seen as a great achievement, when I passed the eleven-plus. Friends and neighbours stopped Mum and me in the street to congratulate us. Auntie Chris and Uncle Bill gave me a hockey stick as a reward, only to discover that grammar girls played Lacrosse. We exchanged it for a tennis racket at the sports and toy shop in the Upper High Street, after learning that most girls left their 'Lax' sticks behind when they left school, so there were plenty going begging.

At the time the results from the eleven-plus came through, Mum was cleaning for Mrs S, who lived in one of the 'big houses' on Woodcote Side. The lady of the house didn't go out to work like my mum, who was managing a family of seven plus two part-time jobs. I couldn't work out why Mrs S didn't clean her own house, or what she did with her time. She had just one daughter, Martha, who was in the sixth form at Rosebery. Mum took me to work with her one day in the school holidays. We stopped for coffee after we had done the upstairs – emptying bins and dusting for me, hoovering and cleaning the bathroom for Mum. The kitchen was huge. There were heavy brown cups and saucers and a bowl in the middle of the table filled with brown sugar lumps. Sugar in our house was white, loose, and spooned straight from the bag, except when Nanny and Grandad McCarthy came round, when some was poured into the basin that matched the ivy leaf teacups, kept in the sideboard for special occasions. Mrs S came into the kitchen, and Mum made her a coffee. 'Maria has got into Rosebery,' she said. Mrs S froze, eyes wide, then squeezed out a 'Well done,' barely disguising her horror that her cleaning lady's daughter was going to be at the same school as her own daughter.

Out of concern for my Catholic soul, being at a non-Catholic school, I was sent to a Saturday morning class for children in the same situation. There were only two of us in the 'group', Fiona and I both having moved from St Joseph's to Rosebery. It was held in the living room of a young couple who lived in one of 'the posh houses' on Pine Hill. Contrary to Mum's standards of poshness, which involved fitted carpets, the room we met in had a smaller-than-room-sized rug laid on parquet flooring. Our leader was a nervous young man, prematurely balding, who appeared never to have conversed with pre-teen girls before. He spoke softly, and had trouble meeting our eyes as he did so, working from a glossy book produced for just such groups, and playing us songs like Simon and Garfunkel's 'I am a Rock' to spark discussion. It was the definition of awkwardness. I attempted to liven up the sessions by chattering to fill the silences left by our leader and my not-so-chatty schoolfriend, but it made me feel tense, and before long I stopped going, leaving Fiona to endure it alone.

Mum was not concerned that I chose Saturday morning telly programmes over sitting in a living room with a rug that didn't meet the edges of the room. Dad neither knew that I had been going to the group, nor that I had stopped, leaving any arrangements to do with his children to his wife. He often took private, cash-in-hand building jobs on a Saturday morning, before going to the pub and the book-ies in the afternoon, so was unaware of any change to my comings and goings. He did, though, ensure that we all went to Mass on Sunday, Mum avoiding church duties, as she was 'far too busy,' with the dinner to cook and clothes to iron for school the next day. Sunday night was also bath night, with three girls' long hair to detangle after washing.

Whilst Dad went to church every week, he never took a seat in the body of the church, preferring to stand in the porch area where the newsletters, prayer cards and holy medals were displayed, viewing proceedings through glass, and leaving as the congregation went up to receive communion. As we got older, and joined him at evening Mass, he would leave as soon as The Rising Sun opened, leaving us to find our own way home. We were forbidden to walk through Rosebery Park after dark, which was the shortest route, but often the sisters would run through, with an eye out for any strangers that might be lurking to catch children out after dark.

I continued to enjoy church in my first year at Rose-bery, if only for the fact that I sang in a children's choir, Our Lady's Singers, having joined while at was at primary school. It was at choir that I kept up with my friends from Irish families that hadn't joined me at the grammar. On Sundays, we wore blue satin sashes with silver fringes, which hung from left shoulder to right hip. They were sewn by our choir mistress, Mrs Field, and her daughter Rosemary, a highly-talented musician who played the organ to accompany us. We were paid 50p to sing at weddings, where we had a bird's eye view from the choir loft as the bride went down the aisle to Rosemary's fingers flying as she played Widor's Toccata in F.

We were collected in Mr Field's Wolsely for choir practice on a Monday night, far too many children than was safe tumbled in the back seat of the car and crouching in the footwell. We sang in the music room of the Fields' home, with French windows open to the garden in the summer, gathered around the grand piano as Rosemary played. This was followed by orange squash and chocolate biscuits in the entrance hall, which was as big as our living room at home.

The Fields had a kitchen and a breakfast room, plus a television room, which was only used to watch the news. I discovered this as I was invited to the house outside of choir practice. Rosemary lacked the company of other girls, as she was home-schooled, and she and I became friends. The Fields took me to musical performances, many of which were dull piano recitals in village halls. The most memorable outing was to hear the children's choir at Brompton Oratory in London. The choir could not be seen from where we sat, so I stared up to the vaulted ceiling, bathing in the heavenly sounds of pure voices. A transcendent experience, which has stayed with me as a visual and aural memory.

To my knowledge, there was only one other girl from an Irish family in the whole of my new school, a girl in the year above me. We had been classmates at St Joseph's, until I was held back to do an extra year due to having a September birthday, and not reaching the age of eleven on time. I bounded up to her on my first day at Rosebery, but she didn't seem keen to renew our friendship. Perhaps it was about being seen with a girl from a lower year. Despite the Houses, designed to encourage girls from different years to mix and to compete for house points, girls from different years didn't socialise. Her voice sounded different than when she was at St Joseph's. She'd held a little of the Irish lilt of her parents before, plus a not-quite-London accent that those of us that lived in commuter towns south west of the capital shared. Her accent was now blending with the girls at school. It was as if she was learning to be English.

I was an outsider amongst my former friends from primary school, and an outsider amongst the children on my estate, many of whom thought little of grammar school girls. Our school summer dresses, a strangely-shaped bottle-green motif on a cream background, was described as 'snot and spunk' by the girls who went to Lintons Lane, the secondary modern. I was also an outsider at school. Not only as an Irish girl, but as a working-class child. Singled out by a second-hand uniform, by the house I lived in, by the fact that my mother cleaned the family house of a girl in the sixth form and, for a while, was a cleaner in the school.

In truth, I had always been a bit of outsider – bookish, inclined to sit indoors whilst my siblings played outside, and a child who loved to listen to the talk of the women who gathered in my Mum's kitchen. I would huddle in a corner, on a stool by the coke boiler, in the hope that I wouldn't be noticed, trying to work out what a 'prolapse' meant, or why it wasn't 'the done thing' to invite the milkman into the house, and what it meant to pay your milk bill 'in kind', like Mrs So-and-So up the road. The talk would suddenly hush when I was noticed. My mother would say, 'Little ears are flapping,' and send me out to play. Looking back, I was gathering material for stories that would not be written for another thirty or forty years.

I couldn't have written those stories at the time; we were not allowed to talk about what went on in the family outside of the home, let alone write about it. In any case, 'What I did at the weekend' was a thing of the past by the time I went to Rosebery County Grammar School for Girls. English was about literature, with creative writing taking second place. We did have rough books, though, with pale blue covers. I covered mine with collages, words and pictures cut out of magazines, protected by clear sticky-backed plastic. I was free to write what I liked in my rough books, as no teacher ever looked at them.

In the Second Form, I started to learn German, and keenly took up the offer of a pen friend. Elke and I corresponded for years, and we exchanged small gifts at Christmas and birthdays. One year, she sent me a page-a-day diary with a dark green mock-leather binding, and so began a daily writing habit, with the next year's diary also a gift from Elke, this one with a cloth cover with a Chinese figure on the front. My mother had no respect for privacy, opening and reading any letters that came into the house, regardless of the addressee. She might get to read my letters before I did, but there was no way I was allowing her access to my innermost thoughts. I kept my diary with me at all times, and slept with it under my pillow.

These diaries, kept in my teens, survived into adulthood until, in fear of others ever reading them, I burned them in a garden incinerator. How would they read if I had them now? There were accounts of unrequited love, of seeing a boy I fantasised about, though we never spoke or met. He stood at the window of his office every morning at the time that I passed, on my way to college. I wondered if he waited for me, if he liked the look of me, too. There were weather reports, too, of the year it snowed at Easter, when the football pools panel met to decide the likely outcome of matches that had been postponed. There were unhappy entries of family tensions, and accounts of my deep sorrow when my older sister left home. I was so confused at the time, and felt her loss deeply, even though she was only a few miles away. We were not on the phone at home, and talking to her meant a walk to the phone box with a handful of two pence pieces. In truth, some deeply important accounts were omitted from the pages of my diary. I truly feared if my mother were to read it.

My experiences were not that different from other second-generation Irish children growing up in the 1960s and '70s. Irish jokes were bandied about, Irish people seen as thick, and, at a time when the IRA was active on mainland Britain, Irish people were either seen as terrorists, or supporting terrorism. When news of IRA activity came on the radio or TV, my Mum would say that all Irish people would be blamed, that things would be said to those of us with Irish accents and Irish names, attacks even. I mocked her for it; I couldn't believe people would be like that. I remember her pained expression, as if I had betrayed her.

In 1974, when I was fourteen years old, the IRA bombed two pubs in Guildford, not so many miles away from where we lived. A few days later, my Physics teacher said to me, in front of the class, 'I see your lot have been at it again.' So began the slow dissolution of the Irish girl I had been. It was safer to pretend I wasn't Irish, so I began to model my identity on my English schoolfriends.

I didn't tell my parents what the teacher had said to me; I didn't tell anyone. I just decided that it would be safer to hide being Irish. I stopped going to the Irish dances, stopped going on the trips 'home' to Ireland in the summer, and showed little interest in things Irish. I suppose it was put down to teenage obstinacy, or the influence of 'that school'. My mother was proud of my place at grammar school, but at the same time put every transgression down to, 'Ever since you've been to that school...'

Dad continued to have scant knowledge of my comings and goings, and if he was hurt or disappointed in my move away from my heritage, he never spoke of it. As Seamus Heaney was to write, the following year, 'Whatever you say, say nothing.' There was a pattern of not talking about troubling things in our family. Keeping my pain about my identity to myself was much like not bothering to go to Mum with a cut knee.

It was not until forty years later that John, my older brother, told me of his close shave with the Guildford pub bombings. As an apprentice toolmaker, he was a day release student at Guildford Technical College, and it was his habit, on college days, to go into one of the pubs targeted by the bombers. The only reason he survived that day unscathed is that he missed college as he had the flu. He also told me of being beaten up outside a nightclub by some 'friends' after Earl Mountbatten was killed by the IRA in 1979. My mother was right, about the dangers of being Irish in Britain. John kept that quiet at the time, too: 'Whatever you say, say nothing'. When asked in recent years if he felt he was English or Irish, he said English.

The letter from Thames Polytechnic, asking me to confirm my A-Level results and my place, had been opened by Mum while I was away in the summer, working in St Ives with my friend Julie. I found it, stuffed with other post, leaflets and bills at the edge of a worktop in the kitchen, soon after my return from Cornwall at the beginning of September. It was a week after the final date to confirm. Mum had not told me about the letter, and looked away as I burst into tears after reading it, busying herself with cleaning the sink. I ran to the phone box on Epsom Common to phone the college; it wasn't too late after all. My place was safe, and they gave me details of the Halls of Residence at Avery Hill in Eltham, Southeast London. Mum did not seem pleased.

A week after my nineteenth birthday, I left for college. I waited in the hall with my bags for Uncle Martin to drive me to South East London. Neither parent was at home when I left, and my goodbyes were shouted into the living room, where a couple of my siblings were watching television, and didn't disturb their viewing to wave me off.

Martin cheerily helped me with my bags when we arrived at Avery Hill, and having checked out the bar, the refectory and my room said, 'There, you have everything you need.' I took my page-a-day diary with me. I stopped writing in it soon after I met the man who was to become my husband, during Freshers' Week. I didn't write again until I was forty.

Freed from the restrictions of home, my boyfriend and I shared my single bed in the Halls of Residence. He slept deeply. Unable to settle on a narrow strip at the edge of the bed, I often took to a sleeping bag laid on the rug on the floor. When he wasn't staying over, I woke in the night, homesick, and missing the shape of my sisters in neighbouring beds. I had never slept alone in a room before then.

I went home every other weekend, and soon realised how unbearable life was there, with Dad's drinking and Mum's moods. By Sunday evening, I felt like a wooden toy with a large key in my back, wound tighter and tighter and not releasing until well into the train journey home. Mum would never say goodbye, or 'Have a good week.' Instead, she would sit in her armchair by the fire watching telly, not even turning her head as I left. I carried the guilt of abandoning her and my younger siblings into my new life at college. It felt like I was being punished for leaving.

I had to clear my room in Halls over Christmas, and a friend with a car helped me do so. There was nowhere to put my stuff at home, as the bedrooms had been moved around: Mum and Dad taking the larger room that had been the girls'; my younger sister taking their old room. She didn't want a second bed in her room, so I had nowhere to sleep except the sofa. I was working on the Christmas post, and had to be up early, waiting until the rest of the household had gone to bed before stretching out with a sleeping bag and pillow.

Christmas Day dawned. We were all too old by then to be up at four to open our presents, as used to be the custom, so I had a reasonable lie-in on the sofa. Presents were unwrapped, and before long the girls were drafted into the kitchen to help with the dinner. Mid-morning, Pam and Dave from across the road came round for a drink, along with their children. Dave looked up at the clock, which had stopped some years ago, but remained above the fireplace. 'What I like about that clock,' he said, 'is that it's right twice a day.' Everyone laughed, as they did every time he said it.

'You must come and see my Montevideo, Mary,' Pam said, proud of her gift from Dave, a porcelain shepherdess, by Capodimonte, it was later discovered. Mum flitted in and out as the glasses were refilled; there were potatoes to peel and turkey to prepare, and a trifle to make. She rarely drank, as if to balance out my father's consumption of alcohol, and rarely relaxed when there was company at home. John Conlon arrived at 11.00, after the neighbours had left, and he and Dad had a couple of whiskeys before setting off for the White Horse. John Conlon had come round every Sunday morning, for as long as I could remember. He smoked, but refused to use an ashtray, preferring to flick ash into the turnups of his trousers. I would watch every week, afraid that his trousers would catch fire.

The men gone, the dinner preparations continued, Mum growing redder in the face, and more snappy and particular as time went on. Her offspring were tasked with setting the table to exacting standards, with the best cutlery and glasses brought out of the sideboard. Potatoes were roasted and mashed, there were great piles of vegetables, Yorkshire puddings, and last of all gravy, decanted into a gravy boat. The meal was scheduled for a quarter past two, giving time for Dad to walk home after the pub had closed. We were all seated at the table, except Dad, who fell in the door late. 'Will you sit down, Jim,' Mum said, but he staggered into the toilet first, and kept the meal waiting longer. All were to collect their plates in the kitchen, except Dad, who was served by Mum, who never sat down to eat until everyone else had a full plate. The tension built as Dad took his seat. 'Three sheets to the wind, as usual,' Mum said, placing a well-loaded plate in front of him. He folded his arms and his head began to nod, his face drawing closer to his plate. He then held his breath, and I waited the longest time for him to breathe out with a snort. 'Come on,' Mum urged us, 'eat up or the dinner will get cold.' She circled the table with a gravy boat, pouring the thick meaty juice onto our plates; onto Dad's plate, too, though he was fast asleep. There were tears in her eyes and she began to sob. 'The gravy's lumpy,' she said.

My boyfriend had gone home for Christmas, but returned to his shared house in Plumstead before term started, so I escaped to stay with him for a few days after Boxing Day. My sleep was no better than in my room in Halls, as he too had a single bed. After that Christmas, I knew I could never live in my family's home again, and never returned for college holidays after that.

My boyfriend and I moved into a flat in Plumstead, South East London, on May 4th, 1979; the day that Margaret Thatcher became Prime Minister. I didn't vote, as I was busy moving my belongings from the Halls of Residence to the flat, and have blamed myself ever since for Thatcher's rise to power. I was in no way politically aware at the time. My parents never voted in UK elections, though I do recall Mum opening a letter from John's Trade Union, and returning a postal vote, her choices based solely on names that took her fancy.

My first opportunity to vote, in a by-election in Epsom, had been wasted on pop-impresario Jonathan King who stood as an independent candidate in our true-blue constituency where neither he, nor any party other than the Tories, stood a chance. I was hoping for a summer job at King's record company, UK Records, and asked him at the hustings if there was any possibility of work. He was dressed in a suit and sneakers, his hands in his pockets, flanked by boys of maybe fifteen or sixteen years old. His answer was a firm no. There were no vacancies. Being female, I escaped a nasty fate. In 2001, King was sentenced to seven years in prison for sexual assault on seven boys aged fourteen and fifteen years old. No one questioned King's retinue of young boys during that election campaign. Though I felt uneasy in the man's presence, detecting something wrong but intangible about King and the boys at his side, I still placed my vote in his favour. An act of rebellion against the status quo, rather than a well-considered vote.

My boyfriend became my husband in 1980, the week before I began the final year of my degree, and nine days before my twenty-first birthday. Our wedding reception was held in the staff social club at West Park, the psychiatric hospital where my mother worked. We had arranged for 'Appy, a DJ we knew from Thames Poly, so-called for his sunny disposition, to entertain the guests. The Irish relatives requested songs he neither knew nor owned, and 'Appy looked less fitting of his nickname as the evening went on, apparently pleasing only the younger guests with his choices. My new in-laws left as the music began, having travelled from Lincolnshire that morning, intent on returning the same day. Many from my side of the church had travelled from County Clare and the Irish outposts of Acton and Orpington, where several of my mother's siblings had settled. They had no intention of stopping the party after the reception ended, moving on to my parents' house to rattle the windows with music, singing and dancing till the early hours. It was ever thus, after weddings and parties; sleeping bodies to be climbed over in the morning before Mum began a morning-long fry-up to feed the hangovers, and then the men would go down to the White Horse for the hair of the dog at lunchtime. This time, I was not there to witness the aftermath of the after-party, having spent my wedding night in a local Trusthouse Forte hotel before heading to the Isle of Wight to start our married life.

Some forty years later, Angela, my brother's girlfriend

at the time, told me that she'd witnessed Mum getting angry with Dad as he'd lost £300 in cash sometime during the wedding day. Whether this was to pay the caterer or cash collected as wedding presents, we shall never know, both parties to the row being dead by the time Angela told me the story.

Throughout our marriage, we would visit my in-laws in Grantham, the hometown of Margaret Thatcher, whom they had seen around town as a child, 'Her nose in the air,' according to my mother-in-law. Mrs T's early snootiness did not prevent Mrs B from supporting the Conservative leader and her government, nor did it stop the in-laws from pronouncing judgement on people who they deemed responsible for the ills of the nation. 'We never liked the Catholics,' Mr B said. The couple held similar opinions about people who lived in council houses and working mothers, who were responsible for juvenile delinquency. As a recovering Catholic, brought up in a council house, and a working mother, I was not what they had hoped for.

Both Reg and Win had come from humble beginnings, but unlike my own parents rise from poor Irish backgrounds, there was precious little expenditure on alcohol and none on gambling, which is how a great deal of my dad's earnings were spent. Leisure spending was alien to them, as was paying anyone to do work that they could do themselves, or throwing anything away that could be mended. Reg and Win had scrimped and saved, and had their own bungalow built after returning from a few years in India where Reg had helped set up a factory to make road rollers with the engineering firm Aveling Barford. As migrants themselves during their time in India, they returned home with little understanding of those that remained in poverty either in India or in England.

I tried to fit in at Reg and Win's, to be the daughter-in-law they wanted, but if I stated disagreement, it made for an uncomfortable atmosphere, so I bit my tongue. I once raised a discussion about the miscarriages of justice around the Guildford Four, the Maguire Seven and the Birmingham Six. My mother-in-law said, 'They must have done something wrong to be arrested.' My husband, who liked to avoid conflict, said not a word to back me up, but on the drive back from a visit, we'd stop at South Mimms services for a drink, and while our daughters ran around the play area, we would offload all the tension, quoting the outrageous comments we'd absorbed over the weekend. 'Have you got lots of coloured people near you? The rough ones.' 'Those people in the council houses across the road … they take off all the inside doors, and keep coal in the bath.'

I can't say that my mother and mother-in-law became friends, but Dad and Reg got on well on the rare occasions they met. They got on famously at my eldest daughter's christening, finding common ground, as Dad had done National Service in Lincolnshire, Reg's home county. The British Tory engineer, who cycled home for lunch from the factory every day to eat with his wife, and the Irish labourer who also worked hard, back-breaking work, but spent more time in the White Horse than with his family.

My husband found my family hard to cope with. They were boisterous, argumentative, and the TV or radio were always blaring; in his family home, you could hear the clock ticking on the mantelpiece. I did not fully belong in either world; however much I had tried to learn to be English, I was still an Irish woman. My introverted husband just couldn't assimilate into an Irish family. My mother complained to me that he never joined in, just sat quietly in the corner. There was no room for shyness or difference in the McCarthy household.

Fast forward by several years. I am in my early thirties, and for the first time since my teens, I am returning to Ire-

27

land, to my mother's hometown, Ennistymon in Co. Clare. My sister is driving, our children in the back. In the years since my last visit, she has lived in Dublin and returned to Surrey. She holds an Irish passport. 'You've never had any interest in Ireland,' she says. I clam up at first, feeling judged, attacked, and then I tell her what that Physics teacher said to me. It's the first time I've told a soul. It's a release, to talk to my sister about being an Irish girl in an English school. She had gone to a Catholic secondary, surrounded by second-generation Irish kids.

Everywhere I go in Ennistymon, people claim me as a cousin. My daughters love the freedom to wander, which they don't enjoy at home. My husband sits quietly in the homes of cousins, aunts and uncles while all the chatter goes on around him. A family wedding is being planned, and he whispers to me that he doesn't want to be around for that. He can't stand all the fuss. Sure enough, his wish is granted, as our marriage ends before the date of the wedding, and my daughters and I attend without him.

'How could you?' my mother-in-law writes, several pages handwritten on small sheets of paper arriving by post soon after she discovered I wanted to end my marriage to her son. 'You've got a lovely house, the children, a car, and you can afford a holiday once a year…' All good reasons to stay together no matter how dead the relationship. We had followed my in-laws route to happiness: saving to get a home of our own, foregoing fleeting pleasures in favour of the security of bricks and mortar, been good parents to our children, worked hard at everything except our own relationship. Never throwing caution to the wind for an expensive meal out, just the two of us, never living beyond our means.

My own mother didn't say 'How could you?' but was nonetheless aghast at my decision. My husband had not abused me, nor had he neglected his children in favour of the pub. Why would I want out?

My parents were endlessly unhappy, but stayed together. Dad had all his practical needs met in exchange for the money from the little brown envelope that he handed over in the kitchen on a Thursday night. Apart from that, he was free to do as he liked, stay out drinking and gambling whenever he wasn't working, and until the money ran out. Mum stayed for appearance's sake, concerned about what others would think, and because she feared the poverty that would ensue as a single parent. Having grown up poor, having a man with a steady wage was of great importance. She stayed because 'You need a father,' as she often said to her children. She stayed because she wouldn't have known what else to do, no matter how bad it got. I once raged to a psychologist about Mum deciding to stay with Dad, when the worst of his transgressions was revealed to her. The therapist said, 'It's her job, what else would she do?'

There is much I could write about the years after my marriage, or between marriages, as it turned out. I became seriously ill months before my fortieth birthday: a breakdown of my mental and physical health, which left me virtually housebound for several years. There was a long estrangement from my mother, and a reckoning of who I was and who I am. Much of what was behind this is not my story to tell. The story that *is* mine is one of confused identities, of not knowing where I belonged. I had moved from a working-class Irish childhood to being the first in any generation of my family to gain a degree, to being a middle-class home owner. I had been a married mother of two, then a single parent; I'd been an Irish girl, who denied her culture then tried to find it again; I had been the manager of a small mental health charity, a job with a great deal of responsibility, then illness took that identity from me, too. I remember sitting on the stairs at home, saying to a friend on the phone, 'I don't know who I am anymore.'

I had thought the support I had always given my family of birth would be reciprocated when I became ill, but that was not to be. Mum still phoned me with her troubles, her awful memories. I was physically too ill to hold the phone or talk for long, and mentally unable to cope with listening to her. I had suffered a lifetime of my mother's emotional demands. Whether her behaviour was due to a chemical imbalance, or the effects of poverty, hunger and neglect in childhood, she relied on her children not only for practical help but to offload dreadful stories from her childhood in Ireland, and for support against the man she always referred to as 'your father'. He drank, he was absent – either at work or in the pub – and when he was home there were quiet resentments between them, which brewed into rows with days and weeks of silence following; rows that that were never resolved.

My father died a year into my illness, and three months after my work contract had been terminated, as I was no longer able to carry out the duties of the job. The phone calls didn't let up; dealing with Mum's grief as well as her usual emotional demands was not leaving me any space to mourn. She was also grieving the daughter I had been, and wanted me back to my old self. Eventually, I asked her to leave me alone for three months, which became years, and although my guilt was tremendous, my health started to improve. Though the dreams continued – of me carrying my mother around on my shoulders, unable to put her down. It was the weight of my mother's dreadful stories, her awful childhood, her loveless marriage, that led to an estrangement that lasted for eighteen years. The phone calls with some awful tale, told once and never mentioned again, finally stopped, though there would be the occasional angry phone call from her. Once she called to tell me what a terrible mother I was; I challenged her own parenting and told her to fuck off. The calls ended, and I moved house a couple of years afterwards, without giving her the new address or phone number.

If my mother told me dreadful things, then Dad told me little. He rarely spoke about his childhood. I didn't go to his funeral; I was too ill, and angry with him for his failings as a father. Any grief I felt was buried beneath the crippling illness that had taken over my body and mind. I was grieving for the life I'd lost – my work, my social life, my quick mind, and the dashing about I used to do.

Whenever my energy allowed, I walked from my home, along the banks of the River Medway, and over the bridge that crosses the river at Rochester. Every time, I stopped at the steps on the bank near the bridge, imagining descending, step by step, into the river, until the water covered my head. My dreams were of drowning, a hand reaching down at the last moment and pulling me to safety. I wore a Claddagh ring on the third finger of my right hand, given to me by my mother when I was young, bought from a kiosk on Limerick Station. An Irish symbol of love and loyalty, often given by a mother to her daughter, the circle of silver had softened and distorted. One morning, I passed the steps without pausing, and close to the foot of the bridge I cast the ring into the water.

Soon afterwards, the writing began. I was with a friend, in a branch of The Works, in Lewisham, and I was admiring a notebook: A5, spiral bound, with a picture of a parrot on the front. 'Let me get that for you,' my friend said. It brought me back to school rough books, the red Silvine notebooks I'd filled as a child, and my page-a-day diaries from my teens, mine to fill as I wished.

I started a distance learning course in computer skills. One of the exercises was to write some text, save it as a document, then reopen it, change the text, and save it as another version. No text was suggested. I sat in front of the Amstrad and thought, what do I have to write about? I don't have a job, I have no purpose. And then the poems began. Poems that took me back to early childhood, to the prefab where I was born, to the radio that sat on a high shelf in the kitchen, to the night my youngest brother was born, to material I continue to mine until this day.

With the small amount of energy I had, I could draft a poem in my notebook one day, type it up the next, edit by hand another day. The poems grew in number, the notebooks filled, and it became a superstition that I could only write in notebooks that were given to me, and they had to be A5 spiral bound.

I had some early success in writing competitions. Looking back on my work from that time, it was a wonder I had the bravado. The poems, the stories, would never get past my 'maybe' folder these days, but there must have been something that the judges picked up, a raw potential. A short story competition won me a place on a creative writing certificate course at the University of Kent, with half my fees paid and a £100 book token.

It was a huge effort to get to the weekly classes for the Certificate in Practical and Imaginative Writing at Bridge Wardens College in Chatham Historic Dockyard. I had hardly left the house for two years, and the classes were at a time I would usually be asleep, during the afternoon. I was terrified each time I entered that classroom. The woman who had managed a small charity for seven years had all but disappeared. The woman who had run training courses, seen clients, negotiated with funders, she was gone. An identity stripped, and a new one, as a writer, yet to be forged.

After the certificate course ended, one of my tutors invited me to apply for a part-time MA in Creative Writing. I was on Income Support at the time, a single parent of teenage children. A friend helped me to apply for funding from charities, for my fees and travel to get to the course in Canterbury. I bumped into my ex-husband in Tesco. I told him that I was taking a course, that I'd got some funding from the Lawlor Foundation, a charity that helped students from an Irish background. He sniffed and stared at the floor. 'Oh, you're Irish now, are you?'

During the MA, I submitted a pair of linked short stories about an Irish mother and her English-born daughter. My tutor wrote on the manuscript: 'This has legs. And more than anything, you need to discover where you have come from.' A third story emerged, with the same, and an expanding set of characters. And even more for my dissertation, all of which formed the basis of my collection, *As Long as it Takes*.

All this time, I was hardly in touch with my family, only with my younger brother. It was a mark of a deep separation that I didn't tell my family of my successes: my writing, the university courses I had taken, both of which I passed with distinction.

In another act of bravado, I sent a piece to the editor of BBC Radio 4's *Home Truths*. A reply came back the same day from the programme's producer, Karen Pirie. 'We don't usually take unsolicited columns,' she wrote, 'but the editor likes your piece. Do you have any broadcasting experience?' Crossing my fingers behind my back, I said that I did. I'd been interviewed on local radio a couple of times, to do with the work of the mental health charity I had managed. It turned out I had a knack for it, writing and recording for broadcast; although the pieces I submitted were edited, the recording sessions needed little direction from Karen Pirie. They were, though, conducted in the least glamourous manner imaginable, in a 'studio' in County Hall, Maidstone, in the photocopier room. Just a desk with a set of headphones and a microphone, connecting me to the BBC in London.

So began a brief radio career as a columnist, writing and recording two pieces of exactly five minutes length when broadcast, in the final few weeks of the life of *Home Truths*. The second column I recorded was about growing up in an Irish family in England. When it was broadcast, I felt a deep pang of loss for the brothers and sisters I no longer saw. I gradually got in touch with them, one by one, after five years of separation, and sent them a link to the *Home Truths* webpage with my photo, taken on the Cliffs of Moher, and an audio clip of my column. I was still going by my married name, Maria Bradley, at that time, and decided not long afterwards to reclaim my Irish surname.

A year later, and seven years after my father's death, I made my first trip to Mitchelstown, his place of birth, and the town he lived in for the first sixteen years of his life. I had become more and more curious about my father's history, about that side of the family. In the time that had passed since my father's death, my anger towards him softened. He had been a cold, distant father, addicted to alcohol and gambling, guilty of sins of omission and commission, which affected his entire family. But once, he was an innocent baby, a beautiful child. What had happened to make him the man he became?

As children, the McCarthys had little contact with the Cork branch of the family, even with our paternal grandparents, who lived only a few miles down the road. Our mother repeatedly told us that our father's relatives were all dreadful. She said that they were cold and unfriendly, and she often told stories of the various crimes they had committed against her. She'd been left standing on the doorstep by one of Dad's cousins, when she and one of my siblings arrived in Mitchelstown, unannounced; Nanny had told Dad that he didn't have to marry Mum, even though she was 'expecting'; Nanny had complained about a mark left on the wallpaper by the baby's arm, when they had briefly lived with Mum's in-laws when John was small; our grandparents favoured their daughter and her children, and didn't care about any of us. Estranged from Mum, I was free to make my own investigations, to form my own opinions.

Contrary to Mum's warnings, I received a warm welcome in Mitchelstown. The story I pieced together on that trip was that my father, conceived out of wedlock, had been left in Ireland when his parents fled to England. He was raised with four cousins who thought that he was their brother, until a man came to visit who was introduced as 'Jimmy's father'. His mother never returned to see him. Perhaps the pain was too much for her. Ireland's history is steeped in secrecy and the shaming of women who became pregnant outside of marriage. Even though my grandparents married before my father's birth, and stayed together until my grandfather's death in 1980, this would not have erased the perceived 'sin'.

When my father was sixteen, he was sent to England to live with parents he did not know. That had always been the arrangement; that his parents would send money for his keep until he left school, and he would then be sent to live in England, regardless of his wishes. When he arrived, he was to meet a year-old sister, who never lacked the love and attention of his parents, which he had been denied.

I took an A5 spiral-bound notebook with me on my first visit to Mitchelstown, and began a sequence of poems about my father and the town he grew up in. Several short stories grew from that trip, too. My Irish heritage, which I had buried for so long, became my writing obsession. My father had been an outsider in the home where he was raised, an outsider in his parents' house, and an outsider as an Irishman in England. He was effectively estranged from his parents as a child. I became estranged by choice.

On that trip to Mitchelstown, a new friend, Liam, told me of his friendship with the writer William Trevor. Trevor was born in 1928, in the same year and in the same town as my father. He left Mitchelstown at the age of five; in all probability, he and my father would never have met. Yet they shared an attachment to the town where they were born, Trevor being more of an outsider due to being in the Protestant minority. Liam told me that Trevor often returned to the town and would sit on a bench in the town square, looking towards the Galtee mountains, watching the kind of small town people go by that appeared in his stories and novels.

Being an outsider is so much a part of my journey as a writer, too. As a teen of Irish heritage, I tried learning to be English, cutting off from the Irish part of me. But you have to know where you have come from to know where you are going; to know who you are.

It was not until estrangement from my family of birth that I began to write, and to delve into where I had come from. I could not have written or shared that writing if I was still in touch, and still there are problems about making my writing public; still there are those who do not want the family secrets spoken of, or published.

I have cycled in and out of estrangement. Since the death of our older brother, John, relationships amongst the four surviving siblings have fractured, fallen apart. The things that held us together now divide us. Perhaps to be a writer, to be fully myself, I have to do so alone.

I have an Irish passport now, and continue to straddle and struggle with my cultural identities. I long for the homeland of Ireland, in which I have never lived, and have an uneasy relationship with the country where I was born and raised. This is best expressed in 'Completely', the final poem of the Mitchelstown sequence, which appears in my first collection of poetry, *strange fruits*:

> I'm Irish with an English voice
> English with an Irish heart,
> Floating forever between
> Holyhead and Dun Loaghaire,
>
> An Irish girl, and English woman,
> not half and half: completely.

Mitchelstown – a sequence

I   The road to Mitchelstown

Suitcases were suitcases then:
large and square, with plastic grips.

They could only be carried a few steps –
one shoulder stooped,
the other raised –
then dropped, hands flexed,
and picked up again
as on the road to Calvary.

So many years I've held the memory
of sailing to Dun Laoghaire
with my mother,
left with the luggage
while she searched for something lost.

Ireland rose in the morning
after the cold crossing on the open deck
of the Hibernia: a passage of women
and children in new clothes,
bags for beds, jackets for pillows.

Once we reached my mother's home
each relative, school, old house, gravestone
was visited and venerated
like the Stations of the Cross.

The suitcases were lighter coming back:
gifts of clothing we'd outgrown
passed on to younger cousins.

This year
I pack four new pairs of knickers,
four of socks, one for each day,

as was done for me
when my clothes were mixed
with my brothers' and sisters'.

Though it's taken all of my forty-seven years
to reach my father's birthplace,
it's all too easy now I'm on my way:

no rise and fall of the ferry,
no full day's travel from Euston to Holyhead,
Holyhead to Dun Laoghaire,
Dublin to Clare;

it's less than an hour by Aer Lingus,
baggage checked at Heathrow,
returned on the carousel at Cork.
It's like eating Easter eggs
without living through Lent.

I wheel my suitcase behind me
and take a seat on Bus Eirann,
from the Parnell Place Coach Station,
Route 8 to Mitchelstown.

My father found the strength
to lift his bags off at this stop
just three times in over fifty years.

I bear no gifts, only photographs
to show those who might remember,
may know what I wish to learn.

I don't know yet if my luggage
will be lighter or heavier
on my return.

II My father's house

'My daddy lived here.'
I lean towards the boy
who shelters in his father's shadow.

We perform the photographic ritual,
standing by the door where he once stood,
the same height as this child.

Two rooms, turf fire, one oil lamp.
Water carried in barrels by donkey and cart.
There are extensions now, bedrooms, kitchen, bathroom.

'I was reared here too,' says Nellie,
gripping the hand of the younger man.
'Your grandfather taught my grandfather to dance.'

'Poor times,' says Jimmy
behind the steering wheel
where he has remained since driving us here
at twenty miles an hour,
worried by the new road that cuts
through Carthy's burreen,
unused to roundabouts.

Flying out and flying home,
an empty seat beside me.
Flying home and flying back,
He's let me have the window.

III   Not even trying

Some speak well of them
as they would of the dead.

'Presentation Convent' wrought in iron
spans the gates in a half moon,
and a plaque commemorates the order,
moved on in favour of new development –
a cinema, a leisure centre –
the rooms behind the boarded windows
haunted by just four women at its closure.

Were they the good ones,
the balance on the scales?

Their children learnt the petitionary prayer:
Please God, not me. The child in the next chair,

afraid to raise his hand, afraid to not raise his hand,
beaten for getting it wrong, beaten for not even trying.

IV   Windowless
There was light enough that night.

I can only guess
if my great aunt's hair was red,
her dress blue or brown
as she stood at the foot of the town
in the heat of the patriot's flames,
not knowing that children to come
would tell her tale to a newfound cousin
with vowels like the Kingstons
who had crowned an Irish town
with an English castle.

Built in the image of Windsor,
'Just one window less',
I am told more than once,
wondering how the light came in,
mistaking it for 'windowless'.

V Two women

We searched the stones
for names that matched our own.
Two women, just met, in the graveyard
of the Church of the Immaculate Conception.

'They'd money to build in spite of the famine,'
you said, nodding towards the date engraved
on the tower: 1847.

I told you of my recent find,
a certificate of baptism.
'My father was a "bye child",

raised by his mother's sister.'
A similar fate
had befallen your grandmother.

The unwed mothers fled:
one to England, one to America.

We entered the church together,
new-found companions,
English-Irish, Irish-American,

descendants of the country that dispersed
its fallen women to one of three destinations:
England, America, the sisters of Magdalene,

and I pictured a girl at the altar,
offering her child
to be cleansed of Original Sin,

handing him to her sister.
Leaving.

VI   Completely

My blood is vintage Irish
but my accent is a giveaway:
Chatham, South East London, Surrey,
with sounds of Counties Cork and Clare.

At grammar, university,
I learnt an English history –
the coming of the railroad,
the growth of industry –
came lately to the famine road,

yet I'm steeped in Latin Credo,
a dose of mea culpa, Agnus Dei,
and choruses of rebel songs
performed at home,
withheld from English company.

In my twenties I received an
English name, swallowed it whole
like the body of Christ.
In my forties, spat it out –
learnt to sign as myself again.

I'm Irish with an English voice,
English with an Irish heart,
floating forever between
Holyhead and Dun Laoghaire,

an Irish girl, an English woman,
not half and half: completely.

* * *

Crocks

i.m. Reg and Win Bradley

Deep dish pies with pastry stretched over domes
of stewed gooseberries, Kilner jars of plums
suspended in pale fluid, towers of tins,
bags of flour and sugar. On the highest
shelf, a marriage's worth of crockery.

Tucked beneath the counter of the pantry,
a tiny larder fridge, packed with butter,
milk, bacon, sausages, for our visit,
the dates ringed on the calendar.

Reg helped in Win's kitchen when he retired,
pea-podding, bean-stripping, washing dishes.
'Men don't wash the pots nicely,' she'd whispered,
inspecting plates as we cleared the drainer.

I held my tongue during tirades
against benefits scroungers:
in stereo when Reg and Win
got bees in their bonnets;
solo after he'd gone.

I remember the day the shelf collapsed,
the crash of crocks as the bracket released,
the painted wood sloping from high to low
in a way that Reg would never have tolerated.

Broken shards of Indian tree platters,
tureens, gravy boats, creamers, in a mess
of dried goods on the oblong of vinyl
flooring that Reg had laid the year before.

His gardening coat and deerstalker hat
hung still on their hook by the back door,
as if he would rise from the table,
put on his boots and go digging.

Home Truths

Uncle Dickie was a great musician and raconteur, but the powers of speech and playing the accordion have left him, with only a few words persisting: his wife's name, Cosima, being one of them. When I visit him in a nursing home in Ennis, he tries to speak my name, but can only manage, 'Mmm, Mmm, Mmm,' his eyes filling as I say a muffled goodbye from behind my facemask, an essential barrier for visitors, two years into the pandemic.

It's the first time I've been 'home' in twenty-four years, the last trip being for the wedding of a cousin, who is now divorced. I call Ennistymon home, as every summer in my childhood and teens my mother, my siblings and I made the long journey from Epsom, Surrey, by train via Euston to Holyhead, then on to Dun Laoghaire by ferry, from there by train again to Limerick and onwards to Clare by bus or taxi, to a place that felt like home, even though we only stayed there for two weeks a year.

My mother was born in Ennistymon at the outset of the hungry thirties, in a room in the attics of Ennistymon House, a big house owned by the Macnamaras, whose youngest daughter Caitlin would later marry Dylan Thomas. My grandfather was a Thomas, too; that being his Christian name. He was caretaker and gardener for the Macnamaras, and when my mother was small, she was given a doll by Caitlin, a story she often recounted.

Eventually, my grandparents were granted a house by the Macnamaras, presumably because the family had grown too large for the attics, my mother becoming the eldest of fourteen. Twelve of the siblings survived infancy. The two that died, at the age of two, were twins, Lulu and Lena. I have only just discovered that my mother had twin sisters. For most of my life, I haven't known the order of birth of her siblings, only that she, Mary McCarthy, née O'Halloran, was the oldest, my Uncle Jerry the youngest, and that both are now dead. At the time of my visit, in May 2022, four siblings are still alive: George, Tommy, Bridget and Dickie, three of them having returned to Ireland after years of living in England.

I stopped going 'home' in my late thirties, after an estrangement from my mother, and because I became very ill, and consequently poor. Also, I knew that she'd be saying terrible things about me, which I had no interest in hearing, or contradicting, while she was alive.

Everyone knew Mum in Ennistymon; she would return to walk the streets of the small market town like a queen. When she went into restaurants, larger portions of food were served than to other diners, or there would be money off the bill. We, her children, called it O'Halloran discount. She was different when in her hometown, more relaxed than at home where we were always on guard against her 'bad moods', her quick temper, her hands ever ready to slap the backs of legs, sometimes with the sting of a plastic spatula from the kitchen drawer, plus she had a sharp tongue that could wound. At 'home', she was the honoured visitor, the matriarch, her own mother having died relatively young, fêted and welcomed in homes across the town: her brothers', her father's while he was alive, May Nestor's, a farmhouse with a large fireplace in the kitchen, with benches inside the nook. As a child, I'd nestle within to listen to tales of the old days, gathering material for the writing that didn't start until my forties, after Mum and I had stopped talking.

Mum wouldn't have liked it, my writing, had she known. It was forbidden to talk about what went on in the family outside of the house. There is a pattern of silence that persists down the generations, backwards and forwards, brought on by too much pain and an aversion to the truth. I relish the truth, but speaking it, writing it, has got me into trouble with my siblings more than once.

Uncle George says he'd know me anywhere. 'There's Mamie, I thought to myself,' he uses a name that my mother was known by only in her hometown. This doesn't sit well with me, likening me to my mother, though genes can't be helped, but I let it pass, only saying, 'You know that she and I didn't talk?'

'Ah, yes, but we won't mention that. We'll leave that on the long finger.'

We sit in McInerney's, an old-fashioned pub that hasn't succumbed to serving food, and has eschewed modernisation, apart from a large television screen that is showing horse racing. My cousin Geraldine, George's daughter, serves behind the bar. She is busy phoning through bets to the bookies on behalf of the clientele. Sitting beneath the screen, I dip my head as a race begins, and all eyes turn in my direction.

George fills more gaps in the family history, adds more stories. I remember Grandad's donkey and cart, which he rode to Lahinch, a nearby seaside town, to play accordion in the pubs for the tourists. He never invited his grand-children for a ride, but then he wasn't the kind of grand-father that played with children. He was more interested in attending the weddings of his numerous grandchildren as we grew older.

'He'd a liking for rum and blackcurrant. Sometimes his lips would be stained black with it. And if he'd had too many … sure the donkey could find her own way home. But the one time, Thomas, your grandfather, he fell off.' George chuckles. 'He said it wasn't the drink, it was the Lady in the Quarry that knocked him off. Now, I don't believe in ghosts, but I had a chill whenever I passed the quarry at night.'

I learn that Linda, George's eldest, was named after Linda McCartney, as both Cousin Linda and Paul and Linda McCartneys' eldest were born in Hammersmith Hospital on the same day. I learn that George nearly lost two fingers in an industrial accident in London, that the quick action of a passing woman saved them, by driving George and the severed digits to hospital. One of his fingers points in an off-kilter direction now. 'I got compensation. £800, which was a lot of money in those days.'

I learn that not only did my grandfather work in Corby Steelworks, but also in steelworks in Scunthorpe, organising groups of men from Ennistymon to join him. Thomas sent money home to his family, which grew nine months after each of his visits. Eileen, my tiny grandmother, died in her fifties. 'It was the smoking that did for her,' George says, though I have no doubt that bearing fourteen children took its toll.

'I remember when she came to stay. It was my job to take her up a cup of tea in the morning, and to read to her from the newspaper that Dad had brought home the day before.'

'Well, she couldn't read,' George says.

'I did wonder… Her hair was pinned up in a bun in the day, steel grey it was, but in the morning, as she sat up in bed drinking her tea, it hung over her shoulders.' It's my only memory of my grandmother. But I do remember that Mum didn't go home for her own mother's funeral, that there was 'no love lost' between them. That we had to have the curtains closed all day, when the news arrived that our grandmother had died, and we weren't allowed to watch telly that day. Mum repeatedly said that she couldn't go home and leave us, the children, but I don't believe she wanted to go. And I don't recall Mum and Nan being in the same room during the visit when I read to my nan in bed. I think I was sent up with the tea and the paper, as Mum preferred to spend as little time as possible with her mother.

What we don't talk about, George and I, is that 'Uncle Guss' was actually my cousin. I am not clear who knows and who doesn't, so I keep my own counsel; keep that on the long finger, as George would say.

It's only later, when Cosima, Uncle Dick's wife, says, 'Guss was Christina's, raised by his grandparents,' that I am free to discuss it openly.

Cosima is an outsider, a German woman who came to Ireland when she was fifty, met my uncle in her sixties when he was busking at the Cliffs of Moher, invited him home to dinner, and so began a romance. They married in their seventies.

Cosima isn't averse to the truth. 'I thought your mother was wrong to ignore you, but she was stubborn.' I learn that Mum told everyone that *she* had stopped talking to *me*, as I had broken up my first marriage. This is as far from veracity as could be, but Mum wouldn't want to cast herself in a bad light, never admitting that she had done one thing wrong in her relationships. And in the years I kept away from 'home', Mum could uphold her position as the returning Queen of Ennistymon, with me cast in the role of the bad daughter.

Cosima can see beyond the lies, listens to my side. 'I could no longer carry my mother's emotional burdens,' I tell Cosima, over lunch in a café in Ennis. 'I was too ill to cope with her. I asked her to leave me alone for three months, which became eighteen years. And though it was difficult – I avoided, or wasn't invited to, family occasions, and Mum wouldn't speak to me at my own daughter's wedding – I don't regret my decision to cut off contact, and I am glad she is dead.' Cosima nods. 'I had to do what was best for me. I was a sick, single parent of two daughters. Mum wanted me to look after her, too, but I put myself first. Therein lay my wickedness, as perceived by her.'

I do not counter Mum's version of events with anyone else I meet on the trip. It's the first time that Cosima and I have met. There's no history between us, and there is a freedom in talking to a stranger. Besides, there are few that remember Mary O'Halloran in Ennistymon now, let alone know of our estrangement and the bad accounts she gave of me. On my last visit, in 1998, when I mentioned her name, that I was Thomas O'Halloran's granddaughter, everyone in Ennistymon would know who I meant. Now it's the names of my cousins that spark recognition when I mention them.

I tell people the story as I travel around Clare, that my mother was born in the attics of what is now the Falls Hotel, when it was a big house owned by the Macnamaras. That Caitlin Macnamara, who married Dylan Thomas, once gave my mother a doll. That Mum was the eldest of fourteen children, that only four survive.

There is a Dylan Thomas bar in the Falls Hotel, and photos of the poet and Caitlin together in reception. There is no Caitlin Thomas bar, even though she was as wild a drinker as Dylan, plus she was a writer in her own right. There is no photo of my mother as a child at the house that she was born in. In another thirty years or so, there will be no one to tell the story of the family in the attic, unless it's carried down through the generations. Perhaps my granddaughter Caitlin will tell it, if I tell her first, of the woman who shared her name, who married a famous poet, and who gave our Caitlin's great-grandmother a doll.

A couple of months after my return from Ennistymon, Cosima sends me a photo of a handwritten sheet of paper, headed: 'List of Children for Thomas O'Halloran and Ellen Coughlan. From 10 – May – 1930 – marriage. All born in Ennistymon, Co. Clare'. Years are listed down the lefthand side, starting at 1931, with my mother's birth, and ending in 1950, with 'Gerard (Jerry)'. My grandmother, whose name appears as Ellen rather than Eileen, as I knew her, gave birth fourteen times in the space of nineteen years.

List of Children for Thomas O'Halloran and Ellen Coughlan. From 10 May 1930 – marriage. All born in Ennistymon, Co. Clare, Ireland

1931	29 June 1931	Birth	Mary O'Halloran	Died 3 March 2018	London, England
1932	10 May 1932	Birth	Michael	Died 29 June 2001	Ennistymon (Gussy's father)
1933	3 June 1933	Birth	Helena		
1934	24 June 1934	Birth	John-Thomas	Died 19 Sept 2019	LMK [Limerick]
1935	17 July 1935	Birth	Tommy		
1936	10 July 1936	Birth	Christina	Died 9 June 2012	Epsom, England (Gussy's mother)
1937	12 July 1937	Birth	Martin	Died 30 June 2010	Acton, London
1938					
1939					
1940			Jeremiah	Died 1940	
1941					
1942	20 Feb 1942	Birth	Bridget		
1943	7 Feb 1943	Birth	Christy	Died 28 Oct 2014	Galway
1944					
1945	15 June 1945	Birth	Richard (Dicky)		
1946	22 June 1946	Birth	Paul	Died 27 Nov 2016	Cork
1947					
1948	16 June 1948	Birth	George		
1949					
1950	12 Feb 1950	Birth	Gerard (Jerry)	Died 2017?	London, England

The list answers some questions, but raises others. There is Helena, born in 1933, with no date of death. Was this Lena, that Uncle George had told me was a twin? And if so, where is Lulu that Mum had told me about, saying that she died at two years old? Was Mum the eldest of fifteen, rather than fourteen? And who was Jeremiah, marked only in pencil: 'Died 1940'? A stillbirth? What is clear is that, by the time my mother was six years old, she was the eldest of six surviving children, and had lost one (possibly two) sisters.

Cosima has recorded that Christina was 'Gussy's mother', and her brother Michael 'Gussy's father'. The biggest secret of all, written down and shared with me. When I was young, we children were told that Guss was our uncle, and at some point (when I was in my twenties, I think), the truth came out. He was, in fact, our cousin, the product of incest, conceived after Christina had returned from years living away in an Industrial School. My guess is that the O'Halloran children had been told nothing about sex, and the proximity of so many children in a small house allowed little privacy. Incest is not unusual when a child has lived away, when siblings have not grown up together. Was it innocent and consensual, or was Auntie Chris raped by Uncle Michael? I only know that Chris was blamed, shamed, and Michael never was.

My mother once told me that her father had gone to the parish priest, desperate because he hadn't enough money to feed his children. The priest's solution was to send some of the children to an 'orphanage', one of the notorious Industrial Schools. Mum came home from school one day to find Chris and Martin gone. She spoke of visiting Chris in Ennis, and seeing this well-fed child walk down the stairs. Mum admitted to me that she felt jealous, as she herself was always hungry.

However well-fed, the regime at the Industrial Schools was cruel, and children who had grown up in them were later compensated by the state. By brother told me of going to a building in Ennis with Mum and Martin, and our uncle burst into tears. It was the place that he had been sent away to as a child.

Eventually, Chris came home to join her family, and when it was discovered she was pregnant, sent away again until the child was born. Guss was raised as if he were my grandparents' child, and Chris went to England, to join my mother in Epsom. She spent the rest of her life in the town, marrying Bill, and having four children by him.

Guss had learning disabilities. He lived a full and interesting life, serving in the Irish Army for a while, discharged on medical grounds. It was surprising that he was accepted, given his limitations. George had told me that Guss was bullied by a superior officer, and became so depressed he'd gone out to the Cliffs of Moher with the thought of ending his life. George had spoken up for Guss, and his medical discharge was arranged.

Guss became the chronicler of the O'Halloran family, with a particular interest in those that served in the army. He published a pamphlet, *The Men from North Clare and the Great War, 1914 –1918.*

When Guss died, in 2019, the parish death notice listed his 'siblings' (in fact his aunts and uncles), and named his grandparents as his parents. Not all his 'siblings' were mentioned; Michael was there, Christina was not. Shamed beyond her death, though the shame did not belong to her.

Guss's house was filled with papers on family history. Once he knew about his parentage, he was desperate to claim his true mother and to be accepted as a sibling by Chris's other children. Uncle George told me that all the papers in Guss's house were burned after his death. A need to clear out things before George's son, Thomas, moved in, or an attempt to erase a shameful secret?

Three months on from the trip to Co. Clare, I am watching Channel 4 News with my husband. A video is playing of an older man playing the accordion. He has been murdered in North London while out busking on his mobility scooter, raising funds for Ukraine. 'Thomas O'Halloran; he's got the same name as my grandfather,' I say. 'Grandad used to play the accordion, too.' I see the video repeated over a couple of days, and think little of it until my aunt, my father's sister, emails me. 'Isn't it terrible?' she writes. She remembers Tommy coming round to play Irish music to her parents, my grandparents, many years ago. I read the message while I am out, and Google 'Thomas O'Halloran': the man that was murdered was my uncle. I feel like I've been hit by lorry. I'm shaking, crying, I feel sick. I message two of my siblings, who had known already; 'We hoped you wouldn't find out,' one of them says.

Suddenly, the small town where my mother and all her siblings were born is all over the news. There is a photo in the *Daily Mail*, taken at Dickie and Cosima's wedding. Tommy sits at the same table as Uncle George, Auntie Bridget and my mother. Uncle George is quoted in the article. The family that lives in Ennistymon is being door-stepped by the press. A journalist sends me a message on Facebook. I have a different surname, but they've made the connection via my cousins. Would I like to make a comment for a tribute to Tommy O'Halloran? I say that I don't want to take part, but the truth is I have nothing to say. I've neither seen nor heard of Tommy for over fifty years. I hardly remember him.

The family are being cagey: 'He wasn't the sweet little old man the press are making him out to be,' reads one message. I press for more information, but no one wants to speak. I remember overhearing a conversation between my mum and dad when I was small: 'Tommy's never coming here again,' Mum says, 'not after what he did.' I saw Tommy just once after that – Uncle Martin took some of us children 'for a spin' in his Mini. He drove us to Tring to see Tommy, his wife and children. I remember it was Tring, as it was the penultimate town in the list of dialling codes in phone boxes. There was Tring, then Truro. Whenever I went to the phone boxes on Dorking Road or on Epsom Common I would look at that list, and think of visiting Uncle Tommy.

Why was Tommy banished from our home? Why was he murdered? Was it a random killing, or did the man know him? Why was he not the sweet little old man the press were making him out to be? Will I ever know the truth? In the absence of the truth, I make up my own stories. Then a half-heard report on the radio one day, as I am preparing dinner. I go to my laptop to check, and there is an email from my aunt. She says there is a piece in the *Daily Mirror* about the trial of Lee Byers, the man that killed my uncle. Byers has pleaded guilty to manslaughter by diminished responsibility. A random act by a tortured soul with severe mental health problems. I have some sympathy for him. We are spared a long trial, and a week later, Byers is given an indefinite hospital order, and is sent to Broadmoor. A few days later, the story has left the headlines; today's news is tomorrow's fish and chip paper.

I write about the dead knowing that my words cannot hurt them now. But the dead leave people behind – brothers, sisters, husbands, wives, nieces, nephews, children and grandchildren, who may not want their stories told. I cannot keep these truths, half-truths, unknowns to myself. It is through silence and secrets that pain and trauma pass down the generations. It is through silence and secrets that wrong-doers move on to other places and carry on doing wrong. Better the 'shame' of public exposure than having your mother's name erased from your death notice, like my cousin, Guss. Better the truth about why Uncle Tommy was never to be allowed back in our house, than to have him lauded as something he was not.

My mother had a habit of falling out with people. Before she stopped talking to them, she would tell them 'a few home truths.' Her truths, the way she saw them. Some of these people, she never spoke to again. One of them was her sister, Christina. Were Mum's 'home truths' anywhere near the truth, or did she say those things to hurt her sister? I had seen her do so years before; tell her sister something so hurtful that Chris fell to the floor of our kitchen, a checkerboard of vinyl tiles, maroon flecked with grey, grey flecked with maroon. I watched, frozen, as my aunt lay screaming, kicking her heels on the tiles like a toddler having a tantrum, her own toddler sitting crying on the floor beside her.

The truth, as I see it, is that none of the O'Hallorans grew up well, or grew up at all. Mum was stuck as the six-year-old, already the eldest of six; the child that never had a childhood. Chris as the girl that was sent away because her parents hadn't enough money to feed her; was sent away again when she became pregnant by her brother. Chris could never find happiness within her family of birth, as her big sister was stuck as the girl who had visited Chris at the Industrial School, and was jealous because Chris looked well-fed while she was always hungry.

I have updated Cosima's list, adding Tommy's date of death, August 2022, and next to the entry for 'Richard (Dicky)' I have added, 'Died January 2024'.

Villanelle at the Falls Hotel

Ennistymon, Co. Clare

We sip drinks in the Dylan Thomas bar
of the Falls Hotel, where Caitlín once lived.
My mother was born in the attic here,

Grandad, the MacNamara's caretaker.
Dylan and Caitlín hang out with us, framed,
As we drink in the Dylan Thomas bar.

Stories once passed from mother to daughter;
the doll that Caitlín gave her, as a child.
My mother was born in the attic here.

Caitlín was a writer and a drinker,
her husband more notoriously famed.
We sip drinks in the Dylan Thomas bar.

No bar named for Caitlín MacNamara;
tales of her family and mine remain.
My mother was born in the attic here

and several children more to caretaker
Thomas O'Halloran, his wife Eileen.
We sip drinks in the Dylan Thomas bar.
My family lived in the attic here.

*i.m. Thomas and Eileen O'Halloran, and their first born
child, Mary*

The spit of him

Home in Ireland, at a house my cousin
was looking to buy – ramshackle, like the one
my mother grew up in. She couldn't imagine
why someone would choose such a thing.

She folded her hands across her stomach,
set her mouth in a line: the spit of her father.

Each time we left at the end of a visit,
he'd stand at the gate, his hands
joined over his belly, his parting line,
'I'll be dead the next time you come.'

I whipped the clothes off her

my mother's retelling
of the quick thinking
that saved my skin.

I remember reaching
for the handle over-edging
the table, tipping, scalding,

Mum's hands pulling
dress, vest, knickers, stripping
fabric before it fused to flesh.

So careless of Auntie Christina
not to place it further in,
to take her coffee black.

Typical.

My mother's finest hour; the heroine.
I stripped her off and hosed her down.
Me, naked in the backyard, shivering.

Twenty Dogs Are Running – Learning Irish on Duolingo

'You have fallen into the demotion zone,' says the little green owl on the screen of my phone. I have eleven hours to add to my XP to stay in the Pearl League. I'll just do fifteen minutes practice. Forty minutes later, wrist and finger hurting from prodding the screen to put words in the right order, I am in fourth place! If I stay in the top seven, I'll be promoted to the Obsidian League again.

I decided a couple of months ago not to compete, just to do my daily duty, learning *Gaeilge* (Irish) on Duolingo. I fell from Obsidian to Pearl, from Pearl to Amethyst, but kept my 200 day streak. Yet here I am chasing glory, hoping to achieve a virtual silver medal, as I did once before.

It began with a poem I read in *The Stinging Fly* magazine, with an epigraph stating that there are only eighteen letters in the Irish alphabet. As a sexagenarian second-generation Irish woman, how did I not know this? When I was a child, some Irish was spoken at home by my parents, the odd word or phrase, but apart from knowing that *bainne* is milk, and phrases that I heard, but never saw written down, I questioned none of it. I never asked what they meant; I simply wasn't interested.

When I read the poem, I was due to travel to County Clare in a few months' time, to my mother's childhood home. Maybe I could learn enough Irish to at least read road signs in *Gaeilge*. Which have the English translations beneath.

Eight months on from my first lesson on Duolingo, some phrases stick, but they are not particularly useful. *Tá fiche madraí ag rith* – 'Twenty dogs are running' being one of them. Other phrases include the Irish for 'My wife left me because she was with another man', and 'My father drinks too much.' The latter would have been useful, were my father not twenty-two years dead; perhaps it will come up when I master the past tense. I've not found a use for the former.

It's a trial and error system, so those words and sentences that you get wrong are offered repeatedly, and some I consistently get right. I am constantly asked to pair words from two columns: *Stobach* with stew, *anrath* with soup, and Duolingo has a fixation on certain animals, too, so I shall forever remember that *portan* is crab. These words and phrases do, at least, stick. Then I am confounded by the need for an additional g before a noun, or an h after the first letter. Sometimes *portan* is *phortan*; I don't know why, but it has something to do with the word that comes before, if it ends in a vowel. I think.

I had hoped that, by now, I would be able to understand some of poems in translation in *The Stinging Fly* magazine, *Gaeilge* verso, before reading the *Bearla* translation, recto. But in a recent edition, all I could pick out was the word *agus*, meaning 'and'.

I was a good linguist at school, learning Latin to O-Level, French and German to A-Level. The teaching methods were entirely different from the repetition, competition aspects of Duolingo. We had slim vocabulary books where we listed words in class to by learned by heart for homework.

By heart ... now hearts are needed to start a new lesson on Duolingo, four of them, and you lose hearts if you make too many mistakes. Or lose heart. You can earn practice hearts if you get thrown out of a regular lesson, correcting your mistakes, and being tested on *stobach, anrath,* or *Tá fiche madraí ag rith* for the umpteenth time. Or you can wait four hours until your hearts are full again.

School taught us French, German and Latin grammar by the chalk and talk method that was prevalent in the

1970s, supplemented by Language Lab sessions for the living languages, with reel to reel tapes and headphones to practise aural and oral, by ear and by mouth. There was practically nil by mouth nor ear in Latin classes; the lessons were dense with grammar and learning by heart. I was off sick the week they covered transitive verbs, and was too reticent to ask when I returned. I never found out what they were in time for the O-Level exam, but somehow I muddled through.

The key to passing was learning by heart, a test of memory. There were passages of Virgil's *Aeneid* to translate, and another text about Hannibal crossing the Alps with his elephants. The translation element of the exam was not unseen; it was a case of regurgitating the translations we'd covered in class and for homework. I only got twenty three per cent in my Latin mock, then crammed before the real thing, committing the entire texts in Latin and English to memory, like chanting the words of a well-known song, or being able to recite the full Latin Mass, having sat through it enough times. Little of what I learned was retained, as I emptied my head of one subject before cramming it with gobbets of Shakespeare for the next, but it worked. I achieved a grade B; not through mastery of the language, but being blessed with a good memory.

Learning by rote has stuck for German. *Mit, nach, von, zu, aus, bei, zeit, gegenüber, entgegen*: prepositions requiring the dative. I thought that some rote learning would work with Irish. So I bought a slim notebook, and wrote *Gaelige* on the cover. My first mistake. I corrected it to *Gaeilge*, and began to write down some of the sentences that came up in my daily Duolingo lessons. I also bought a second-hand copy of *Learning Irish*, by Mícheál Ó Siadhail, as recommended by my brother's partner, Radu, who had used an online version of the book when learning Irish ahead of a trip to Ireland, to supplement Duolingo. The book arrived mottled with damp and draped in threads of cobwebs. It made me sneeze, so I awaited a replacement, and also ordered an Irish-English dictionary, which turned out to be the tiniest one available, a Collins Gem, inscribed with the name of another Maria: 'Maria Napier, Class 11C'.

Duolingo offers no grammar as such, so I hoped that Ó Siadhail's course would help me out. There are lists of vocabulary for each lesson. I transcribed the words and their translations in my slim notebook. There are grammar pointers, too, and the first thing I learned was 'Irish has no indefinite article. "A man" is simply expressed by *fear*.' Confusing to the beginner, the word *an* indicates the definite article; so 'the man' is *an fear*. The grammar is mainly illustrated with phrases and sentences. I tested myself with the exercises at the end of Lesson One. I did badly. No problem, I thought; it would be like cramming for the Latin exam, repetition and committing to memory. I read the chapter again, noting things down, and retook the test several times. On no occasion did I score more than three out of ten.

I gave up on the book after Lesson Two, though I do remember some of the vocabulary I learned by heart, and the possessive that added an h to the name Cáit in the phrase *cóta Cháit*, Cáit's coat. Though I am not sure whether the use of the possessive brought this about, or the fact the preceding word ends in a vowel.

So, back to Duolingo, but supplemented with some YouTube videos, Learn Irish with Dane, which offer such things as days of the week, months, seasons and numbers, with the benefit of an Irish speaker presenting, so as to get a better idea of pronunciation, which often bears little relation to how words are spelt. I used the videos to make lists at the back of my slim notebook, with the rest of it for writing down tricky phrases that I just couldn't get right on Duolingo, which offers the correct translation, moves on, then comes back to the one you've got wrong, after you've forgotten the weird strings of vowels within new words, or as single letter words, with or without the *fada* accent. It was at this point that I realised that you could tap underlined words on the screen, and be given a translation. Facepalm. It's not always the correct translation in the context of the phrase, and though several words can be offered, often none of them are correct.

The algorithm is unforgiving. With a hard-copy teacher, 'They are working' would be as acceptable as 'They are doing work', but not with Duo, the little green owl, who sometimes will only allow, 'They do be working.' Sometimes Duo will let a typo pass, or a missing *fada*, thankfully the only accent to learn in Irish, like the acute in French. Other times, Duo throws you out of the lesson for a single mistake.

Then there are the adverts. I have the free version of the app, so must endure dog food offers (I don't own a dog), ads for insurance companies and charity donations, and games to install on your phone. I disdainfully told my other half that I don't play games on my phone. Then I realised that's exactly what I had been doing for months, chasing after XP, working through Levels, earning crowns and medals, competing in leagues. Reader, I had become addicted.

When I learned Romanian on Duolingo, ahead of a trip to Romania, I picked up enough to order *cafea cu lapte*, to say *mulţumesc* when my coffee was served, and to recognise the women's toilets – *Femea* – from the men's – *Bărbaţi*. My friend, who had taken no Duolingo lessons, bought a Berlitz phrasebook, and fared better than me. Between us, we ordered all the tickets for a complicated series of train journeys through Transylvania from a ticket office in Sinaia, where no one spoke English. Let's be honest; she ordered the tickets, and I said *mulţumesc* when they were handed over.

Romanian does, at least, have roots in Latin and Germanic languages, so I had a starting point; unlike Irish, which seems unconnected to anything I had learned before. I stopped my Romanian lessons after the trip, and thought I would do so with Irish, after our holiday in County Clare.

I wasn't going to do my daily Duolingo duty whilst on holiday, but just fifteen minutes a day wouldn't hurt. Some days, our exit from the Airbnb was delayed by my need to learn a little more, to do 'just one more lesson', or by the offer of double XP for the next fifteen minutes. I was delighted when I knew that *go mall* means 'slow', before reading the English translation on a road sign. And I entertained my husband with loose translations of the inscriptions on the gravestones in the cemetery on Inís Oírr. 'That's his wife, and his son is buried with him, and *fuair bas* means died,' I said, as I worked through the sad lists of children who survived only hours, days, or months. Due to my YouTube lessons, learning Irish with Dane, I translated the months of their deaths: *Bealtaine* – May; *Meanmeath* – June; *Fómhar* – Autumn; *Nollaig* – December, or Christmas. From the words *Dia* and *t-anam*, I worked out 'May their soul rest with God.' My husband's enjoyment of our trip to the Aran Islands would surely have been diminished without me as a guide.

Wandering round Kilkee, I saw a shop sign: *Siopa beag, bróga agus éadaí*. 'I know what it means!' I said. 'Little shop, shoes and clothes.' The husband insisted on telling the women behind the counter that I had been learning Irish, and that I had translated the name of her shop. 'Go to the top of the class,' she said, in English, and though she then spoke slowly and carefully to me in Irish, I couldn't understand a word she said.

Alas, I never got the chance to use the phrase *Tá fiche madraí ag rith* while in Ireland, since at no point did I see twenty dogs running. I saw a lot of cows, but the Irish translation for that animal has not come up on Duolingo.

In the months following my return from County Clare, I couldn't quite kick the Duolingo habit. There's a lost heritage at stake, having if not denied then ignored being Irish during my teens and twenties, the victim of internalised anti-Irish racism. The language drives me crazy, though there is a sudden enlightenment when I work out a word or phrase used by my parents fifty or sixty years ago. I had no interest in learning their meanings at the time, thinking only, 'Dad's speaking Irish again.' All those times he said, '*Oscail an doras*,' and none of his five children obliged by opening the door. The dog only responded to 'Give me the paw,' never to, '*Tabhair dom do lámh*,' literally, 'Give me your hand.'

There are some remembered phrases that Mum and Dad spoke, which I can only remember phonetically, and they remain a mystery. If I carry on learning Irish for just a little longer, maybe one day I'll be able to translate them. But, for today, I am trying to not take a lesson on Duolingo, for the first time since I started learning. If only to prove that I am not addicted, and it really doesn't matter if I fall down to the Amethyst League.

As a postscript, I have stopped taking daily Duolingo lessons. In the process of writing this piece, I realised I was addicted to the app: all Duolingo leads to is more Duolingo. I am not convinced that it's the best way to learn a language. I now get to read all sections of the Saturday *Guardian* before it's time to buy a new one, and I am spending more time writing. There may be a time when I will return to learning Irish, but I shall try a different method. Or maybe I'll complete the Open Learn Philosophy course that I abandoned when I took up with the little green owl.

The Wild Atlantic Way

The windsculpted trees
of the Burren bow, burdened
like shawled old women

Flashes of yellow
draped with seaweed fingers grip
in the limestone grikes

A rucksacked hiker
strides straight-backed, rainhood drawn tight
heading for Fanore

The caramel cows of County Clare

The colour of an Everlasting Toffee Strip
they melt into fudge if licked.

Feasting slowly on the deep green,
their milk falls as soft brown cream,

swirled by sudden Burren rain,
churned by Atlantic winds.

From Norah to Noreen – a never-ending story

A companion piece to the story 'More Katharine than Audrey', which you may want to read first.

I grew up with a knowledge of mental illness: of people locked in large institutions and of those who cared for them. My mother worked as a nursing assistant in one of those institutions, two nights a week. She brought home stories about patients who should not have been there in the first place, or had suffered short bouts of mental ill health thirty or forty years before, and were never released.

I remember going to a Summer fete at West Park, the hospital where my mum worked, seeing the extensive, well-kept grounds. I remember, as an adult, giving her a lift to work and walking the corridors with her to the ward; long, glass-sided corridors that seemed to run for miles. I remember walking past the laundries with their huge boilers. I don't remember seeing a single patient.

In July 2008, a news story came onto the *Today* programme on Radio 4 by the reporter Angus Stickler. It was about women typhoid carriers who were locked away in a mental asylum, Long Grove Hospital in Epsom, the town where I grew up. Long Grove was familiar to me as a place where aunts and friends of our family worked, and as a neighbouring hospital to the one that employed my mother. My ears tuned in; the radio no longer a background buzz to my breakfast.

These women, who had contracted typhoid fever, and continued to carry it in their faeces after recovery, were locked away in the sanatorium ward in Long Grove. None of them was mentally ill when they entered the hospital, but they needed to be kept away from a population that was afraid of infection. What place more isolated than a mental asylum in the country?

Before the advent of appropriate antibiotics, there was no cure for typhoid carriers, and the women were effectively condemned to a life sentence in the hospital. Then some were treated and cured. They were released from isolation, but sent to other wards in the hospital. Some of them were, by then, badly mentally deteriorated; some remained lucid. None of them went back to their homes or former lives; none of them received visitors, or had families that inquired about them. In those days, the stigma of having a relative locked away in a mental institution was so great that people just disappeared, and were never heard of, or mentioned again.

Some women remained resistant to the antibiotics, and lived and died in isolation. One woman lived in a single room for the last six years of her life, and remained *compos mentis* to the end, with her only company the nurses, the newspaper and a small television.

I looked on the BBC website and read more about these 'Forgotten women'. There was a list of their names, and a request for information from anyone who might recognise a family member who had disappeared. That list of names made me weep. A former ward manager, Jeanie Kennet, spoke of the women with affection, spoke of them as her 'family'. The women had received loving care from some of the nursing staff, despite their instructions to merely feed and water the women; to warehouse them.

43 women were admitted to the ward between 1907 and 1957: some died, and were marked as 'deductions' in the hospital records; others remained in the hospital until its closure in 1992. Rosina Bryans, one of the typhoid carriers, spent 60 years in the hospital, and was transferred to another asylum when Long Grove closed.

On a trip to Ireland the year before hearing this programme, I met my father's cousins, Nellie and Mary. Dad was raised (or 'reared' as he would say) by his aunt and uncle, Molly and Mick, in Mitchelstown, Co. Cork, and with cousins that he rarely mentioned. My trip, the first to his hometown, was seven years after his death. I had gone in search of the boy that became the man, in search of a missing half of my history. All I knew was that Dad had been left in Ireland as a baby, his parents going to England soon after he was born, and that he eventually joined his parents who had settled in Ewell, near Epsom, Surrey. But not until he was a young man, or child as we would see it now, soon after leaving school. He only returned to Mitchelstown a handful of times, and it felt like there was a deep pain attached to his childhood, which he was never to address, soaking it in alcohol instead.

Cousin Nellie told me of her sister, Norah. Norah had left Mitchelstown, Co. Cork, to go to London and train as a nurse. This was in the 1940s, at a time when English hospitals were advertising for Irish girls to come and train as nurses and work as domestics. Nellie told me that Norah came home to Mitchelstown on holiday, and got into rows with their father. She was out late, dancing, and she wanted to smoke at home, which he would not allow. There was a big argument. Norah went back to London, and was never heard of again.

Norah haunted me: what if she were still alive; what would her life have been like; did she regret her break from her family; was it the making of her; what if she were killed shortly after returning to London, run over by a bus? How easy it must have been, in those days, to disappear without a trace.

In the absence of knowing, we make up our own stories. What if Norah were one of those women locked away in the typhoid ward in Long Grove Hospital? Norah became Noreen, and the story began.

I decided to start writing in the first person, as Noreen, early in the morning, shortly after waking. I was writing in a semi-conscious state, slightly muddled, emulating Noreen's state of mind. I wrote episodes from her current life and from her past, disjointed scenes and memories. Some of these were based on my mother's stories of hospital life, some on other family stories of emigrating from Ireland in the 1940s and '50s . Some details were drawn from the true-life accounts in *Across the Water, Irish Women's Lives in Britain* (Mary Lennon, Marie McAdam, Joanne O'Brien). Bits were added to the story as I saw them, and as they occurred to me. While picking blackberries, I was reminded of doing this as a child, and that my father would never eat them, like Noreen's father in the story. The shabby dress that Noreen's mother wears is identical to one I saw worn by a older woman who was tidying her garden, complete with slip hanging below the dress. The taffeta dress that Noreen wears to dances is one I saw on an antique stall in Harrogate. There was yellow enamel jewellery to go with that dress; it didn't end up in the story, but I knew Noreen was wearing it.

Then came the task of joining these episodes in a way that could be understood, without losing the manner in which Noreen's thoughts jump between past and present, hopes of cure and release, and despair. There was a great deal of reordering, and reading the story again recently, I'm not sure I got it right.

An even greater task was revealing the fact that Noreen is a typhoid carrier. My first attempt was clumsy, ending the narrative with a simulation of the radio interview that Angus Stickler (the reporter on the *Today* programme) conducted with Jeanie Kennet, ward manager. I showed a draft to the tutors on an Arvon writers' retreat, Julia Bell and Martina Evans. Both liked the story, but strongly disliked the ending. More subtle reveals were suggested, and the idea was planted that Noreen was a woman of appetites, and that somehow her appetite should be linked to her downfall.

I went home and did some more research on typhoid: how it is contracted; symptoms of the fever stage; when the antibiotics became available that cured carriers, and why some people were resistant to them. I wove these details into Noreen's narrative: '*Pea soup* it said in the books: *six to eight motions a day, and it looks like pea soup*. That's just how it was when I had the fever.'

I also thought more about Noreen's appetites. She loves women, but is denied fulfilling that appetite, partly because of her own inhibitions as an Irish Catholic of that era, and because there is no indication that Shrub, the object of Noreen's affections, reciprocates her love. There is also Noreen's love of food. The story begins with a list of meals, the way that Noreen marks the passing of the hours and the days in Long Grove. She loses her appetite after Shrub marries, then regains it at the restaurant meal with Sid, allowing him to touch her knee beneath the table:

> but it was the food that got me going, not him. It was all I could do to stop lifting the plate and licking it clean. After Shrub married, I got so thin that my curves all but straightened, but my appetite returned that night. And a hand on my knee beneath the table, which did nothing for me, but I let him.

That night is literally her downfall, as she contracts typhoid from someone working in the restaurant kitchen.

> That was the night that did for me: someone in the kitchen of that restaurant. Someone that was a typhoid carrier like I am now, not washing their hands, passing it on to all that ate there.

Metaphorically, the typhoid is a punishment: not for being a lesbian, but because she is denying her true nature by allowing Sid to make love to her, when it is Annette Shrub that she loves.

> He drew me onto the bed beside him, slipped the

dress from my shoulders and kissed my neck. His face was red; he was breathless. I shouldn't have led him on, so.

Poor Sid – I feel for him, and some readers have asked what happens to him. That is not my story.

Lastly, the title. Some readers have disputed the use of Katharine Hepburn as an unattractive woman as compared to the other Hepburn, Audrey. Noreen's views are mine, as are her favourite films. I have seen *The Nun's Story* (Audrey Hepburn) more times than I can remember. Noreen's reaction is indeed my own:

> The times I saw that film, and each time the tightness in my chest, a hankie at the ready when she goes into that room at the end of the film, to leave the convent, and she gets her old clothes back, the ones she came in with, and there's no one there to say goodbye, as if it's a disgrace, wanting to go back into the world.

As for Katharine Hepburn, I suppose she is attractive, but ugly at the same time. She looks too skinny for her frame in her films. Personally, I have always wanted the gamine frame and look of Audrey Hepburn, but like Noreen: 'I could never be like Audrey Hepburn; my hips are too wide.'

William Trevor rarely gave interviews, but I was fortunate to hear him talk to Mark Lawson on BBC Radio 4's *Front Row* some years ago. The interview has since disappeared from the ether, and as I am working from memory, I can only paraphrase Trevor here. Readers are more likely to remember a story than they are a novel, Trevor said. And short stories can have long lives: they can win prizes, be anthologised several times, published in a collection, broadcast, and. And so it was with 'More Katharine than

Audrey', a story of which I am very proud. It appeared in my collection, *As Long as it Takes,* in 2014; it went on to win the Society of Authors' Tom-Gallon Trust Award in 2015, and was later anthologised in *I Wouldn't Start from Here* (Ray French, Moy McCrory, Kath McKay, Wild Geese Press, 2019). It was one of the stories studied by students at the Irish Writers in London Summer School, 2021. It hasn't been adapted for broadcast, but I live in hope.

Re-reading the story, ahead of my guest writer spot at the aforementioned Summer School, I decided I wouldn't go back and change or add it to it, but the person that inspired it continues to haunt me, and her family, in her absence.

The year that *As Long as it Takes* was published, I was invited to read at a Culture Night event in Mitchelstown, Co. Cork, my father's hometown. The event took place in Kingston College Chapel. As I stepped up to the lectern, I wondered if I had chosen an appropriate passage to read in such a setting. The excerpt concerned Noreen's encounter with 'men's parts', as a young nurse:

> Da thought it was the boys I was after when I went to England. Jesus, with what I've seen of men's parts, what's there to get excited about? Like snails tucked in a hood, and sometimes, sick as they were, it would rear up at the feel of the sponge. God, the first time I saw one at full length I called for Sister. I thought something awful had happened.

An older man approached me after the reading, and leaning forward, conspiratorially, I thought he was going to express his disapproval. Instead, he whispered, 'Your husband must have a good sense of humour.'

My 55th birthday fell during that visit, a day after my father's cousin's Nellie's birthday. By now, she had dementia, and was not as lucid as when I had met her seven years before. I was invited, along with my husband Bob –

the one with the good sense of humour – to a dinner at the Firgrove Hotel in Mitchelstown to celebrate Nellie's birthday. It was there that I met her three daughters – Anne, Edel and Liz – and the celebration moved to Anne's house after the meal, where the wine and the stories flowed freely. Nellie's repeated contributions to the conversation were, 'You're Jimmy's daughter,' (to me), and 'You look like Gerry Adams,' to Bob.

I gave my second cousins copies of *As Long as it Takes*, and we got to talking about Norah, their missing aunt, who had inspired my character Noreen. 'We didn't even know she existed,' Edel said.

'Then I was going over for an interview at a hospital in London,' Liz said, 'and I was going to stay over in Epsom. With your mum and dad.'

'So, just before Liz was due to leave, Mam told us about her sister, Norah. Never a word till then,' Edel said. 'I think she was worried that your dad would mention her, and she wanted Liz to be prepared'

'Well, I never knew a thing about Norah until years after Dad died, so that wasn't going to happen,' I said.

Dad never talked about his childhood; it was a history I was not to discover until seven years after his death. Mum had told her children that the Cork side of the family were stand-offish, unfriendly. A judgement that was not borne out by the welcomes I received on my visits to Mitchelstown. As I get older, I have learned not to take other people's judgements at face value. Even now, I am learning that half-truths were told and secrets kept to suit the family script, to keep us from questioning or finding out for ourselves.

The cousins went on to tell me that their mother, her sister and brother had tried to search for Norah, through the Salvation Army. 'They found someone who they thought was Norah,' Edel said. 'But the woman said it wasn't her.'

'Maybe it *was* her,' I said, ' and she didn't want to be found.'

In the introduction to *An Unconsidered People: the Irish in London*, Catherine Dunne writes of the secrets held by Irish women in England who had children by Afro-Caribbean fathers, a wave of Irish migration colliding with the arrival of the Windrush generation. 'If you couldn't arrive home in 1950s Ireland with a child born out of wedlock, you certainly couldn't come home with a black child born out of wedlock.' The mothers would go home to Ireland for Christmas, leaving the children behind; many grandparents were not even aware of their grandchildren's existence. 'And sometimes the grandparents in Ireland went on not knowing for the rest of their lives.'

In Gus Michael Nwanokwu's memoir, *Black Shamrocks: Accommodation Available – No Blacks, No Dogs, No Irish*, he relates how his Irish mother was completely cut off from her family after marrying a Nigerian man. The punishment for being open about a loving (and lifelong) relationship with a Black man was expulsion. Perhaps some of these Irish women, like Nwanokwu's mother, found it better to initiate the estrangement themselves, and disappear without explanation. Could Norah have been one of those women, rather than the fate I imagined for her as my character Noreen?

My brother John was a taxi driver in his middle and later years, and remained living in Epsom, in the house that we grew up in, not far from the now closed Long Grove Hospital. Ever the proud big brother, John was in the habit of telling his passengers that his sister was an author. Five years after *As Long as it Takes* was published, John told me that he had picked up a passenger who had worked as a nurse in the typhoid carriers' ward at Long Grove. He told this retired nurse about my story, 'More Katharine than Audrey', but failed to remember her name, or get her contact details. I would happily have sent her a copy of *As Long as it Takes*, to receive some feedback from her as to how my imagined world of the closed ward matched reality.

John, rarely seen with a book in his youth, became an avid reader as he grew older. I would send him books that I thought he would enjoy, and always copies of my own publications; he insisted on paying me for them, for the books that bore my name. His comments were often to offer a corrective to facts, like a story in which I mentioned his beloved Chelsea beating Leeds, 2-1, in the FA Cup final. I had got the year wrong, he told me. He phoned me about a poem that featured an incident between John and Mum, where she poured boiling water over a record that he had played on repeat, driving her to distraction. 'It wasn't "Flowers in the Rain", it was : "Hole in My Shoe" by Traffic,' he'd said. What a shame; the former fitted poetically with Mum planting a Busy Lizzie in the wavy bowl created by her repurposing of John's one and only single, played over and over on the newly acquired Dansette record player. He came home from work one day to find his beloved vinyl moulded into a flower pot, sitting on one of the low brick walls that flanked the steps up to the front door.

Having read *As Long as it Takes*, John phoned me to talk about 'More Katharine than Audrey'. He, too, had walked the corridors at West Park Hospital in Epsom, where our mother had worked. John remembered the physical world of the hospital I describe in the story, the grounds, the corridors, the huge boilers in the laundry. He told me how well I had captured it. Knowing that John was so taken by this story is a great source of pride to me. This time, he offered no factual corrections.

Local people had used the corridors and grounds of the five asylums on the outskirts of town as short cuts, or to walk home after nights out when the buses had stopped running. The reception for my first wedding was held in the staff social club at West Park, and our family attended several other such celebrations in the clubs of West Park and the other hospitals.

So many of our neighbours, friends and family were employed as nurses, domestics, in the kitchens, in the laundries, the gardens, and as 'auxiliaries', as our mother had been. 'NA', her name badge read: Nursing Assistant. It was pinned to her uniform every Monday and Tuesday evening before she left to catch 'the break' – the staff mini-bus that stopped at the top of our road – returning early the next morning full of stories. Her charges were always 'the patients', sometimes given cruel nicknames such as 'Flipper', and most definitely seen as 'other' by Mum and her work colleagues. Mum and her work friends were known by their last names – Shrub, McCallion, Connolly. The manager who came round to check on the wards during the night, she called 'Deputy God'. The Nursing Auxiliaries, working in twos, were left in sole charge of a ward of mostly sleeping patients, taking turns to sleep themselves while one kept watch in case of a visit from Deputy God.

There was humour within what were surely grim sur-roundings. The 'patients' were dehumanised in many respects, and perhaps by using only their surnames at work, the staff were able to distance themselves from the dreadful back stories of their charges, and the possibility that, given other circumstances, they too might have been locked away. Mum had undiagnosed mental health issues. Her reluctance to seek help was perhaps due to the stigma of ending up as a 'patient', like her charges.

The last time that 'More Katharine than Audrey' had an airing was when I was invited to be a guest writer at the Irish Writers in London Summer School in 2021. Held on-line, I was greeted before the participants joined the meet-ing by the course leader, Tony Murray, and his partner Joanne O'Brien, one of the authors of a book I had found in an Oxfam shop many years before: *Across the Water: Irish Women's Lives in Britain* (Mary Lennon, Marie McAdam and Joanne O'Brien). A chance find, which had inspired characters and experiences that appeared in the stories in my collection. I was astonished by this chance encounter, and hope that other connections will be made as time goes on.

This story has not reached its end – meaning both 'More Katharine than Audrey' and the real-life stories that inspired me to write it. Norah may still be alive; she would be in her eighties or nineties by now. I think of her from time to time, wonder how her life has been, how it is now.

The fictional story may yet have another life, other lives. I dream of it being recorded, for audio, or as a talking head short film, performed by a woman with the right accent. Fiona Shaw would do. I can dream big. And I expect that Norah and Noreen will continue to haunt me, and be revealed to me in the most surprising ways.

Genealogy

Sweet Joseph Williams, obsessed by his ancestry,
stays for a week at a Mitchelstown B&B
talks over breakfast about genealogy
to all of the guests and the B&B landlady.

There's egg on his jumper, the same he wore yesterday.
working by day, and by night genealogy.

He hitches a lift out to Ballyporeen,
ancestral home of old Ronnie Reagan.
Joe's seeking O'Gormans, his own distant cousins,
then he asks would they give him a lift to Clogheen?

'Must write them down,' he says, 'old people's stories:
they've brains like computers, and excellent memories.'
Looked it all up in the National Library,
working by day, and by night genealogy.

Sweet Joseph Williams is here on his holiday.
His eyes are alight as he talks of his ancestry.
There's some who would hide at his sight, but not me;
I've an ear for his stories, the tales of his ancestry.

I'm just like him, I am tracing my ancestry,
searching the faces of staff in the pharmacy
for someone, a cousin, for someone who looks like me,
adding on branches to my family tree.

'Must write them down', he says, 'old people's stories:
they've brains like computers, and excellent memories.'
Looked it all up in the National Library,
working by day, and by night genealogy.

Sweet Joseph Williams is here on his holiday.
His eyes are alight as he talks of his ancestry.
There's some who would hide at his sight, but not me;
I've an ear for his stories, the tales of his ancestry.
I wonder if he is related to me.

Song lyrics by Maria C. McCarthy, set to music by Bob Carling

On the Stairs

'I believe in fiction and the power of stories because that way we speak in tongues. We are not silenced. All of us, when in deep trauma, find we hesitate, we stammer; there are long pauses in our speech. The thing is stuck. We get our language back through the language of others. We can turn to the poem. We can open the book. Somebody has been there for us and deep-dived the words.'

Jeanette Winterson,
Why Be Happy When You Could Be Normal?

I stand on the landing of the house where I grew up with my mother Mary, my father Jim, and my four siblings. I was the middle child, sandwiched between two sisters, with a brother either end. John, the oldest of us, lived here most of his life, and even in the times he lived away from the house, he never really left it. I don't believe that any of the children of Mary and Jim McCarthy have mentally left that house, but John returned physically, time and again, until he was found dead, seen through the letterbox by his boss after John had failed to turn up to work that morning, the first day back to work after Boxing Day, 2022.

When our father died (who art in Heaven, or more probably in the other place), halfway through the first year of the new millennium, John was about to sign the contract on a shared ownership house; the first home of his own, at the age of 45. 'You don't want to do that,' Mum said. 'Move back here, and you can buy the house from the council.' John later told me that it was the worst decision of his life to buy that house, and to live with our mother for the last eighteen years of her life. He survived her by only four years and ten months, living for some of those with his dog, Rupert, until Rupert left him, too.

John's books stand on narrow shelves of dark wood on the strip of floor where John and Dad played darts, the dartboard on the door of our parents' bedroom. I kept score, standing a few steps down the staircase, trying to add the numbers from the sections of the board that the three darts from each round had landed in, double for landing between the outer two wires, treble for the inner two, and subtract the totals from the previous round. My grammar school maths was never as quick as the mental arithmetic of two seasoned darts players. They always got there before I did, so I simply marked the scores in two columns on a piece of paper.

It's not the same carpet as fifty years ago, when the darts tournaments took place, just the same strip of landing. The books are on the top shelf and half of the second shelf down, and below that a pile of papers. In amongst them, I spot a letter in my handwriting, dated 21 June 2016. It's on blue notepaper in blue ink. The ink fades as the writing travels down the page, no doubt due to an ink cartridge running out. I had placed the letter inside John's birthday card. His 61st birthday was just three days after the date on that letter. I scoop it up, along with half a dozen books; I'll wait till I get home to read it.

The house is cold. The heating has been turned off, and it's one degree centigrade outside. We are not intending to stay long. Bob, my husband, is concerned for me. This is the third time we have visited my childhood home since John's death, after more than twenty years absence on my part. Each time, I have become distressed. He is urging me to return the keys and not to visit again, but I am not yet ready to admit defeat in the face of that house and all that it holds.

I turn from the bookcase to face the top of the stairs and the small window with the deep, red-tiled sill. A goldfish once swam there in tiny circles in a globe of water, a funfair prize carried home in a plastic bag full of water, a brief survivor. Suddenly, I'm watching John running down the stairs pursued by Mum, red-faced and furious, hurling the goldfish bowl after him, John turning to grin as he leaps the last step, the goldfish flapping at the top of the stairs, the carpet sodden, the bowl bouncing to the bottom of the stairs. My arms feel swollen and painful; my hands lock into claws. I am unable to move for a few seconds.

I viewed so many scenes from those stairs, watching myself from outside of my body, a body that felt like it didn't belong to me. I felt invisible to others at such times, and sometimes believed that I could make myself invisible; by staying still and quiet I would not be noticed. When Dad spent weeks ignoring one of my sisters, I watched from the stairs as she followed him through the hallway, a few steps behind, both on their way into the living room. I watched as he entered the room and closed the door behind him, as if his daughter did not exist. I watched my sister's expression, the way she held her body, defiant and broken. Neither Dad nor she was aware that I was watching.

I broke my silence only once, from my place on the stairs. My parents were arguing as Dad stood with his shirt off by the bathroom sink, Mum in the doorway, the beginning of their usual cycle – a row, then weeks of silence, which would be broken by Dad giving Mum some money. I listened for a minute, unnoticed, and then I told Dad that he'd never been a proper father to us. He looked taken aback for a moment, then broke into a smile. 'Why the dramatics?' he said.

I was crushed, but some time afterwards, Mum told me that he'd taken my words to heart, that I had made a difference. Except there was no difference. Nothing changed.

'You really shouldn't come here again,' Bob says. He is keen to get me out of the house and home. We have only come to return files of paperwork that we took home a couple of weeks ago. Apart from his accounts, which were handled by an accountant, John's admin was in a mess. We found a notice of a private pension lump sum, left unclaimed, in with a car service history. There were two notices about safety issues regarding the electricity supply to the house. Other important documents were in old envelopes with supermarket shopping receipts. There is no sign of a will.

We have sorted everything into a concertina file; Bob has made a spreadsheet of everything in the file, and marked action needed. All important documents have been scanned and shared in Google Docs with my surviving siblings, along with the spreadsheet. It took over three hours to sort and read everything, with papers laid out on our dining table and my desk. Even longer for Bob to do the scans and make a spreadsheet. In spite of this, I have been attacked in a family WhatsApp group chat for removing paperwork from the house. 'We agreed that nothing should be taken from the house,' someone begins, before others pile on. Having turned my phone off for several days, I opened WhatsApp to thirty-four messages, most of them telling me that I'd done something wrong.

There is a smoke alarm/carbon monoxide monitor beeping intermittently, but neither of us can bear dealing with it. It would mean searching for replacement batteries, or driving into town to buy some and entering the house again. My younger sister has said that she is coming to the house later, so we leave a note on the stairs so she will see it as soon as she walks in the door. She has left several notes dotted around the house for my benefit, on green A4 sheets: DO NOT TOUCH next to lamps with timer switches; DO NOT TAKE, on boxes of paperwork, some with John's bank statements and accounts. One sign states DON'T MOVE, by a movement sensor that has been placed near the kitchen door, added since John's death to deter intruders. I freeze in a comic pose next to it. None of the cupboards have signs on them, so we open them and throw away jars with quarter-inches of jam in the bottom, and take tins of butter beans, bags of ground decaf coffee, bars of dark chocolate and muesli bars. We also take three Christmas gift bags with bottles of wine in them; it doesn't seem right to leave them in the house of a recovering alcoholic, even though John is no longer around to be tempted by them. One gift is from a regular customer, two from the adult children of an ex, Scott and Sarah, whom he used to live with when they were children. It's strange. He might have kept his drinking past secret from his Evri customers, those he delivered parcels to, but why would he not have told those that knew him well?

I remember John telling me about going to Sarah's 30th party. 'I was tempted to drink,' he said. I asked why he had gone, knowing that he avoided events in pubs and boozy occasions. 'Being tempted and actually drinking are two different things,' he said.

Bob and I mark the bottles for the next raffle at Bob's Urology Support Group. Knowing that John sent Bob cheery messages during Bob's treatment for prostate cancer, calling Bob 'Mr Freeze' after he'd had cryotherapy. John would approve.

I gather half a dozen books from John's shelves, all non-fiction. One is a book I sent him after reading it myself, Alan Johnson's *This Boy*. Johnson's teen years reminded me of my brother's, and I thought John would enjoy it. John's politics were further left than Johnson's, but it was the era and experiences that chimed with me, and I hoped they would with John. The other titles are two by Naomi Klein; *Chavs: The Demonization of the Working Class* by Owen Jones; *Iris* by John Bayley; and *Why be Happy When You Could be Normal?* by Jeanette Winterson.

We leave Epsom and head towards the Wells Estate, to the house where my Auntie Chris and Uncle Bill lived with my four cousins. It was a second home to me, which I would walk to during the long school holidays to spend time with my beloved aunt and cousins. That was if Mum and her sister hadn't fallen out, which they often did for long spells. This meant that we children were also not to speak, and that the usual traffic between the two houses was suspended.

I remember a wedding that both families attended when I was about 17, a couple of months into the current silent battle between the sisters. My dad and my uncle worked together. Dad travelled to work and back in Bill's van. I can't imagine that they held the silence during the working day, or while drinking in The White Horse. But both couples stood separately at the reception. 'I suppose we're not supposed to talk to each other,' I said to my cousin Danny. He shrugged and held out his hand for me to dance with him. We were well practised in rock and roll dancing from previous weddings and dances, and he was soon flinging me round the dancefloor. By the end of the evening, the sisters were talking again, and peace was restored.

This was not to be the last rift between the sisters. Shortly before my own estrangement from my mother, they fell out permanently. I no longer went to family occasions, but I was told by my younger brother that Mum would not acknowledge Chris at their brother Martin's funeral. Chris died a couple of years later, and Mum said that she would go to the funeral, but would not speak to Bill. When word of this came to me, I broke my silence with Mum and wrote to her to say that she should either not go the funeral, or recognise that Bill was grieving and speak to him. Whether my letter had any effect, Mum did phone Bill before the funeral, and I heard that she behaved as well as she was able to on the day her sister was buried.

I took the opportunity in that letter to tell Mum how she had spoiled my daughter's wedding day a few months before. I had offered an olive branch, that we should be civil to one another, for the sake of the occasion, but Mum could not resist making the day about her. She sent a message, via my brother, saying that it would be better if we ignored each other. At the reception, she made a point of passing my table, walking close to where I was sitting, and dramatically sticking her nose in the air. She spent much time linking arms with my ex-husband, and dancing with him. Never having met my second husband before, she spoke to him as he was ferrying bridesmaids and flower arrangements between the place where the ceremony was held and the reception. She must have been aghast that she had inadvertently been civil to Bob, before she realised he was attached to me.

In the days after John's death, I have spoken to one of my cousins, who received the news of John's death from someone in Epsom, before John's siblings had had a chance to let all the family know. Word was going round Facebook, too. No doubt from neighbours who saw the ambulance staff break into John's house. One of my sisters tell me that there is still a rift with that family, but as I have played no part in it, I see no reason to behave other than I used to when my cousins and I were young.

I direct Bob to the house in Well Way where my cousins used to live. The former hedge has been ripped out and the front garden paved over. The road is parked up, but we find a spot. I think about knocking on the door, but decide against it, and on we drive through Ashtead and Leatherhead to reach the M25. Then a clunk, as Bob mounts a traffic island, misjudging the space he had to overtake another car. It's the second tyre that's gone since John's death, the first happening close to home. This time, it's freezing cold, and the nearest place to pull in is the car park of a school. The mobile tyre service can get to us in an hour. We pass the time wondering how much the fees are for the school; their website will offer them on enquiry. Which means if you need to ask, you can't afford them. I go into reception to explain why we're there, and to ask to use the toilet. I explain to the receptionist that I've been to my late brother's house, that we're sorting his affairs. The receptionist is all too willing to help. I am directed to a posh loo with proper towels and fancy hand soap, and she offers me a seat on a sofa and a hot drink. A small act of kindness. I leaf through the glossy magazines, a quiet respite before the journey onwards. I take the burst tyre as an omen. Bad things happen when we visit that house.

We find a recipe that uses butter beans, having taken several tins from John's cupboard. There is a recipe called Jane's Spanish Stew in a vegan cookbook. It uses two types of beans, vegan sausages, tomatoes, peppers, herbs and spices. It's delicious. We make it several times in the coming weeks, until all the tins of butter beans are used up.

I love dark chocolate, as John did, but when it comes to opening the chocolate bars we took from his kitchen, I can't do it. They sit in the cupboard until there is a call for donations to the local foodbank, and in they go. I can neither keep them nor eat them.

John did not crack the spines of the books that he read, as I do not crack the spines of the books that I read. Here is a book he read before I did; I am reading it now. I read the books he read: the word 'read' looks the same written down, but one is active, is happening now, the other has happened and will not happen again. I read (reed) the books that John has read (red) and will not read (reed) again.

I begin reading *Why be Happy when you could be Normal?* It's Jeanette Winterson's memoir of growing up with adoptive parents. The title comes from her mother's comment after Jeanette Winterson tells her that her relationships with women make her happy.

Winterson cannot bring herself to write 'Mother'; instead she uses 'Mrs Winterson' throughout the book. Mrs Winterson is like our mother, mine and John's, in that both had bouts of manic behaviour. For our mother, everything had to be done, and carried on with being done, until it was finished. I am like that, too; I work till I drop. And I did, collapsing into a chronic illness just before I reached 40; an illness from which I have never fully recovered.

Mum's manic activity was in the morning. She didn't stop till lunch, and after that she didn't move till it was time to start the dinner. She had only two speeds: full pelt or motionless. Motionless being in front of the telly, in her chair, near the fire.

I have had my own spells of manic behaviour. Sleepless, up in the night, out walking so early in the morning that I found the barriers to the country park I wished to walk in locked, and when I did gain entrance, a ranger approached me with some concern about me walking alone, head down, hood up, body closed in itself. 'Just be careful,' he said. 'There are some strange people about.'

After the birth of my second child, months after, consumed with grief for Julie, a close friend who had taken her own life the same week as my daughter's birth, I started to strip the bedroom wallpaper, convinced that I could decorate the room in a day. Halfway through stripping one wall, I collapsed.

Not knowing what to do with me, my husband shipped me off to my mother, along with our children. Mum had persuaded me, several months before, that I should not go to Julie's funeral. I wanted to talk about Julie, her difficult life and horrible death, but the only person who would let me do so was another friend, Alison. I thought Julie's death was my fault. She and I had fallen out; if I had just been there for her, she might not have done it, taken the overdose, died in a horrible way over several days.

Mum thought it best if didn't talk about Julie. She took charge of my girls and sent me to buy some new clothes and get my hair done. She showed her granddaughters off to her friends in Epsom High Street, while I sat in front of a hairdresser's mirror, not wanting to look at my reflection, not wanting to face myself. 'Are you going somewhere nice later?' the young hairdresser asked.

'No. I'm having my hair done because my friend killed herself.'

John was not around at the time when Julie died, nor when my daughters were born. He was living in Australia when the first was born, and called me on the communal payphone that stood in the hall downstairs in the flats where we lived at the time. I was so happy to hear his voice. International calls were expensive back then, and usually kept short. He spoke for ages, while my baby slept upstairs. I wish I could remember what he said, apart from the jokey tone. I can only recall telling him I was going for a postnatal check-up. 'Oh no, you're telling me about your body now,' he said.

As for when my youngest girl was born, John was back in England, now separated from the girl he had been engaged to, with whom he had gone to Australia. Drinking had taken over. I don't recall him seeing the baby either around the time she was born, or several months later when I came to stay with Mum and Dad.

In recent years, John and I spoke about Julie's death. He remembered her well – attractive, funny, intelligent, creative. We'd been friends throughout grammar school, and into my years at Thames Polytechnic. Instead of going to art school, as Julie had planned, she began a career as an inpatient in psychiatric wards at the age of 18, being treated for anorexia nervosa. Our time together became visits to her in 'The Unit', the acute psychiatric ward at Epsom District Hospital. I would go to see her whenever I was home from college. How comfortable she looked in the day room where we met, next to the kitchen where she regularly refilled her mug with hot water. How different from her bedroom where we had spent so much time together. She would sit on her bed near the window that framed a suburban garden, trees, lawn and flowerbeds, her German Shepherd dog, Mazda, at her feet. The walls draped with posters and Indian print scarves, records leaning against the music centre, where she would make mix-tapes, recording from vinyl to cassettes. Her long, straight hair parted in the centre falling over her face. Head dipped, smiling, joking, her humour sometimes cruel, directed towards those that we knew.

It was tea that she drank then. With milk, then black, then hot water without tea; a new trick learned from the other 'skinnies', as she called them, as they counted calories together in The Unit. Then they deprived her of visits until she gained weight. A perverted carrot and stick method, if the use of the carrot metaphor was not so inappropriate. She was eating so many of them, to the exclusion of 'fattening' foods, that her skin turned orange. And so she appeared in my friends of the bride photo, on leave from the psychiatric ward with a carotene tan in a loose-fitting smock dress to hide the body she reviled.

When visits to Julie were banned, we wrote instead. I kept her letters for years. Written on Kermit the Frog notepaper, with a cheery green creature waving from the envelope, she wrote of going on 'Loonies' outings' and seemed at first to consider herself an outsider, not one of the 'patients'. In time, Julie became like an old lag in prison. She learned other tricks: as well as drinking hot water instead of tea she was taught more efficient ways to cut her arms. On a visit home, I bumped into Margaret, Julie's mother, outside the hospital. She looked as though she hadn't slept, spoke fast, sometimes throwing her hands up in submission. She didn't know what to do to help her daughter. None of us did.

Margaret told me that it wasn't my fault when we spoke in the days following Julie's death. 'It seemed to do her good, for a while, when you broke contact,' she said. 'She really tried to get better.'

When I told all this to John, in recent years, he agreed with Margaret; there was nothing I could have done. 'She'd tried loads of times, hadn't she? She was bound to do it in the end.' I told him that Mum had prevented me from going to the funeral, and said it was best not to talk about it.

'It was fifteen years before I could grieve. I couldn't believe that she was dead. I kept having dreams of her being alive. If I'd gone to her funeral, I wouldn't have been sobbing to a psychologist fifteen years afterwards.'

'Perhaps Mum was right,' he said. 'You shouldn't have gone.'

A decade after Julie's death, John was admitted to The Unit. His drinking, his drug-taking no longer gave him relief from his mental pain. He had walked into A&E, and told them he'd had visions of his own death. John phoned me from the ward, while I was at work. 'I told myself, Maria will know what to say,' he said. I was working for a mental health charity by then, and was well used to advocating on behalf of service users. John wanted to talk about our home, our family, the worst of it, those things he hadn't dared voiced for fear of breaking the family code of silence. 'I've been used and abused,' he said, having returned to live with our parents after a relationship break up. It was unbearable; it always had been. It had been for me, too. That's why I left a week after my 19th birthday, and never lived there again.

But the hospital staff would not allow John to engage in a talking treatment until he had addressed his drinking, and the rest of it – the dalliance with smoking heroin, the pills. 'I'll speak to someone on the ward,' I said. I was confident that when I said I was a mental health advocate, they would listen. I would tell them that the drugs and the drinking were tied up with trauma, with emotional abuse, that John wanted to talk about it. My name would bring a response with mental health professionals in the area where I worked, as the manager of the advocacy scheme. The professionals would answer my calls, would talk to me. It cut no ice in Epsom; nor that I was John's sister. No one would speak to me.

Mum did not visit John in The Unit. She didn't want people to know that her son was 'a patient'. As a Nursing Assistant in one the asylums in Epsom, Mum saw 'patients' as other, not something with which any member of her family should identify. Dad did go to visit John. Dad, the source of many of John's problems; the model of an alcoholic father. He looked out of the window of the day room. He could see his local pub from where they sat. 'It's a warm evening,' Dad said. 'I think I'll stop for a cider at The White Horse.'

A residential rehab programme was suggested, but John went back to work instead, went back to living in the house that caused him so much pain; that caused all of us so much pain. The fear of speaking out, the terror of anyone finding out that he'd asked for help, the pain of addressing all that stuff that drink and drugs pushed down, it was too great. No doubt there was pressure from Mum not to be telling outsiders our business, and pressure to get back to work, another way of squashing down those things that needed to be dealt with. John could not stop working after retirement age, and often worked seven days a week, delivering parcels. Until he dropped dead.

Fair play to John for (mostly) staying off the bottle by his own willpower. There were no twelve steps for him, no meetings. How much better it might have been for him if he had gone to that residential programme, if he'd left the house he'd grown up in, and never went back. He went to his siblings in times of crisis, our younger brother taking him in one time, finding John a counsellor, whom he saw for a while, until he didn't.

On John's shelves after he died was a book entitled *Toxic Parents*. I didn't take that one; I knew enough about it already.

The letter I found on John's shelves, the one that I had slipped inside his birthday card, is one that John told me he hadn't received. Several months after I'd sent it, we met at our nephew's wedding. I told him about having to sell our house because of financial difficulties, and he knew nothing of this. 'I wrote to you about it,' I said. 'There was a letter in with your birthday card.'

'Oh, things happen in that house,' he said, and looked towards our mother, by then in a wheelchair, and in the grips of dementia, but still wielding power. She had never respected the privacy of her children, opened any letters that came into the house, regardless of who they were addressed to. If she had read and hidden my letter, this meant that John had not received my birthday card.

At that wedding reception, I watched as Mum held court at a round table with her children and grandchildren around her; apart from her youngest daughter who sat at the top table with her son, and her middle daughter, banished to another table far across the room. There I sat with my husband, aunts and uncles of the bride, and the bride's father's girlfriend. The bride's divorced parents sat awkwardly, side by side at the top table, their current partners seated elsewhere. A brother and a sister came over to talk to me, to commiserate at my banishment, but also to report that our mother was 'on transmit', talking without filter, upsetting just about everyone she spoke to. 'She said something so nasty, I can't repeat it,' my sister said.

Mum and I spoke, too, for the first time in many years. I felt pressured, as several people said to me, 'She wants to talk to you.' I didn't want to behave towards Mum as she had towards me at my daughter's wedding, so I made an approach. The conversation was civil enough, but when I told Mum about a planned school reunion, with girls from my class, she said, 'They're all bitches'.

My sister said, 'Maybe she'll let go, now she's talked to you again.' We were waiting for her to die. She hung on for another eighteen months.

I thought at first that John hadn't read the book that I now held, *Why be Happy When You Could be Normal?* The spine is not cracked, though the pages look like they have been turned. There is a rip all the way across page 143, by the line: 'It is a lovely story – Caedmon would rather be with the cows than with people.' I don't think it has any significance, just an over-enthusiastic turning of a page.

There are no annotations by John, no bookmark left in. I don't like to annotate books, either. I have not done so since having to learn gobbets of Shakespeare to regurgitate in exams. I don't know if John ever studied Shakespeare. His schooling ended at fifteen, the last year when children could leave at that age. Not that they were thought of as children then, John going straight into an apprenticeship as a toolmaker in a factory with men three times his age and more.

Towards the end of the book, Jeanette breaks down following her adoptive father's death, which happens during the search for her birth parents. She had found some paperwork relating to her adoption with corners torn off and crossings-out, hidden in a locked chest with Mrs Winterson's Royal Albert china. Mrs Winterson pre-deceased Mr Winterson by several years, and he had remarried and been widowed again. He died shortly after visiting Jeanette at Christmas. Nesta, the owner of the care home where he lived, serves Jeanette tea in a tiny cup:

A tradition in the North of England [...] to show respect [...]

"You'll have to see the coroner," she said. "You might have poisoned him."

"Poisoned my dad?"

"Yes, with a mince pie. The doctor told him not to travel – he comes to you alive – he comes back here and drops dead. I blame Harold Shipman."

I am reminded of a conversation with John as he drove me and my youngest to Upnor Castle. I told him that I liked making lists. He went quiet for a moment, then said, 'Harold Shipman made lists.'

We'd had a nice day, the three of us, walking by the Medway, lunch in a pub overlooking the river, a walk on the foreshore, and a trip to the castle. Then the word 'Mum' flashed onto the screen of John's mobile. He stared at it with a worried expression. 'Don't answer it,' I said, 'You'll be back in a few hours; whatever she wants can wait till then.' But he did answer it, and I could hear what I called 'the voice', wheedling and pitiful; Mum had achieved her aim to evoke pity and guilt, to invade our day. I was annoyed at her games, urged him not to give in to her, but John drove me and my daughter home, and left soon after.

Like Mr Winterson, John died at Christmas. The day after Boxing Day, in all probability, though the coroner marks it as the 28th December, as that is when his body was discovered. I'd sent John a photo of our traditional Christmas morning walk in Santa hats, me and Bob by the

Medway, and he'd replied, 'Happy Christmas, Cookie,' my childhood nickname. He signed off as he always did, 'Love you. John x' That was the last I heard from him.

I write to the coroner, ask that he sends me everything that he is sending to my sister, who is the link person to the four of us that survive our brother. 'There is a history of family difficulties and estrangement,' I write in an email. He responds the next day with a copy of the report. No suspicious circumstances. We are free to arrange a funeral. It will not be until seven weeks after our brother's death.

Jeanette Winterson takes her partner, Susie Orbach, to the house where she grew up for the first time. As I did with Bob, sixteen years into our relationship. These things normally happen in the first flush of love; there is no normal, neither in Jeanette's relationship with her parents, nor mine with mine.

A turned back corner on the bottom of page 201 – accidental, but proof that John had read this far, with only twenty pages to go. Jeanette discovers that Mrs Winterson lied to her about her birth mother, telling Jeanette that her mother was dead.

My mother lied to others about me, and lied about others to me. There is something that chimes with me, in Jeanette Winterson's memoir, about others being the gatekeepers of knowing, of secrets held. The family I was born into is full of secrets. Growing up, things were revealed by accident or deliberately, and there was then the minefield of remembering who knew that secret and who didn't. Even after John's death, the secrecy continued, a sister deciding who should read what amongst John's papers. There were envelopes marked CONFIDENTIAL DO NOT OPEN in her writing. I opened and read them. I do not believe in secrets, and my imagination had run to far worse places than what the contents revealed. A DBS check with details of criminal offences from John's youth, which had to be disclosed for his taxi licence. I fully remembered the police coming to the house and arresting John, the court case held at a seaside town, where John and his mates had got into a fight that summer, Mum going to speak up for him in court. The worry that it would be reported in the local paper. All a long time ago. Why the shame, the secrecy? Why the decision to be the gatekeeper of these secrets?

I began writing about John long before I knew I was a writer. An essay, at school – about my big brother. The teacher described it as 'a lively portrait'. I was in awe of him, but also a little scared. He could be wild, untethered. When I was small, he used to play a game with me, called Elephants. John would sit on me, pin me to the floor, and attack me with a succession of imaginary creatures, beginning with butterflies, ending with elephants, thumping me on the chest with his fists. The thumps were too hard.

I described, in my school essay, how John once brought a girl home, a woman, who was about to get married. He had met her on her hen night. There would have been 'none of that sort of thing going on in this house,' as our mother put it, so the woman must have slept on the sofa. 'Go over the Common if you want to do that sort of thing,' Mum would say, which was ironic, given that was the very place where John was conceived, bringing on a quick trip to the altar when Mum was five months gone.

This girl sat shocked and confused in our kitchen as the Sunday morning ritual of a morning-long fry-up began. Her skirt was short, above the knee, she had long, ash-blonde wavy hair and wore glasses. What had gone on? Had John's infamous charm lured her away for a last night of freedom? Or had she seen that she was sleepwalking into a marriage that she really didn't want? Had John tried to rescue her from a path that so many blindly followed, into early marriage and motherhood?

Neither John nor Mum knew about that essay. Mum

would have been appalled by it, I am sure – talking about the family outside of the house. Some forty years later, John appeared in fictional form, in my story 'Cold Salt Water'. It was based on two of his experiences: narrowly escaping the Guildford pub bombings and being beaten up as the child of Irish parents the night that Earl Mountbatten was killed by the IRA. He loved the book in which the story appears, *As Long as it Takes*, and spoke to me at length about it, knowing that the fiction was based on the reality of growing up in an Irish family, as we had done. But when it came to my first attempt to write non-fiction, from life, John reacted strongly.

I had written to all of my siblings, telling them that I was working on a memoir. It was being written sensitively, based mainly on the complicated grief I had suffered, including when our parents had died and when my friend Julie had taken her own life. I would not be revealing anyone else's secrets, only mine. I wanted to know if I could use my siblings' names, or would they prefer that I use 'younger brother' and so on? I offered to send a sample of the writing. Only one sibling responded positively. The others did not want to mentioned by name, or to appear at all. John became so anxious at the thought of family secrets being revealed that he could not leave the house for several days, and eventually went to see his doctor. I dropped the whole idea, seeing how distressed he became, and became so scared of upsetting the family that I could not write for a year afterwards.

I have come to the conclusion that John held all of us siblings together, that we all felt he needed looking after and protecting, that he was the most vulnerable of all of us. Now that he is dead, the glue has dissolved. Some mask their pain in drinking, drugs, over- and under-eating, shopping, over-working, abusive relationships, helping others while ignoring their own needs. I've used some of these myself. But now, I deal with my pain by writing, and hope that others can find recognition and solace in seeing their experiences reflected in mine.

I am drawn to a quotation from Jeanette Winterson's book: 'I needed words because unhappy families are conspiracies of silence. The one who breaks the silence is never forgiven. He or she has to forgive him or herself.'

I have read just one other book that I took from my brother's shelves: *Iris* by John Bayley. I have wondered why he was drawn to this, a memoir of lives so different from our own experiences. The only connection I found was that Iris Murdoch was friends with the writer Elizabeth Bowen, and spent some time at Bowen Court near Mitchelstown, our father's childhood home.

I wanted more of John's books, and asked that my siblings send some to me by courier, sending money to cover the cost. This was initially agreed, then the money was returned to me, and the books never arrived.

Goldfish

Standing on the landing
of my dead brother's house –
our dead mother's house –
I am caught, as John was not on that day,
by a flash: our mother lobbing
a glass globe, lifted from the red-tiled sill,
aiming at her son as he runs downstairs.
John, quicker than our mother's temper,
turns and laughs as he clears the last step.

Here I stand, fifty years on,
watching once again.
A goldfish gasping
on the soaking stairs.

Flowerpot

When we got the Dansette my brother bought one single, 'Flowers in the Rain' by The Move. He played it over and over. Mum smashed it. He bought another, set it up so the needle went back to the start of the record as soon as it ended. Seconds of crackling silence, then a click as the arm returned and hovered above its cradle, then floated back to the booming start, regular as a heartbeat.

Boiling water moulded the disc into a wavy sculpture. Filled with earth, and planted with a bizzy lizzy, it was there when he came home from work, on the doorstep, a flowerpot catching the rain.

A Mermaid at Upnor

There are fishtailed dolls
in the gift shop at the castle,
and 'Be Mermazing' captions
on magnets, mugs and cushions.

Meanwhile, in a garden
in the cobbled high street,
a mermaid reclines, back arched,
parted lips painted red.

She's seen some action,
this siren, heavy, wrinkled,
curls piled high on her head
like coiled serpents.

And though she's long dead,
I hear my mother speak:
Mutton dressed as lamb. Brassy.
No better than she should be.

Uncles

i.m. Karan Bucknall

Your Uncle Jack is at the wake.
He's telling stories
of my Uncle Jerry,
back in the sixties,
fresh from County Clare
to look for work.

Jerry's gone, too.
More years he had,
my friend, than you.

'I'll always be six months younger,'
my annual joke repeated on each of your birthdays.
Now I'll outrun you, come September,
in a way I never could in the races at school.

Jack's mouth crumples, crooked streams meander
through his work-tanned wrinkles. An unfamiliar
sight in an old Irish workhorse out to pasture.

But now he's laughing, picturing Jerry,
his hair dyed black and quiffed like Elvis.
entering the dancehall, hands on hips,
as if to say, 'Come on girls, come and get me.'

Club Outing

The coach arrives. You are hoping to get on the back seat with your best friend Karan Regan. Your cousin Danny is in the queue, but you don't want to sit with the boys. You think about the time when he showed you his willy, and you pulled down your knickers, so you would know the difference between boys and girls. You didn't tell anyone because you knew it was rude. You didn't even tell Father Chatterton in confession, because he knew it was you, even though the curtain is supposed to disguise you. It would have meant a whole load of Our Fathers and Hail Marys: too much trouble.

You pile on the coach. *Epsom Coaches* is written on the side, maroon on cream, and a printed-paper sign in the front window says: *Comrades Club: Epsom–Littlehampton*. Everyone cheers as the coach pulls away from the Working Men's Club, turns out of Ashley Road and onto the High Street.

The singing starts. The songs are rude, but the grown ups are too busy talking to notice. It starts with 'My husband's a lavatory cleaner', then it's: 'Oh my auntie she's expecting me for tea.' You get to the second verse

Oh she's got a lovely bust of Rabbie Burns

Oh she's got a lovely bust of Rabbie Burns

Oh she's got a lovely bust,

Got a lovely bust

Oh she's got a lovely bust of Rabbie Burns

Then it's the verse about the auntie's lovely country house in Kent. No one sings the really rude word except Terry Blackman, and someone shouts, 'That's enough now.'

The coach parks outside the Littlehampton Working Men's Club, and you queue up for your goodie bag.

There's an apple, an orange, a bag of crisps and a fifty pence piece. It was in old money last year, but there has been D Day since then. D stands for decimalisation.

The dads go off to the pub and the bookies. Mum says she doesn't know why Dad bothers to go to the seaside, as he spends enough time in the pub at home, and the bookies in Littlehampton won't be any different from the ones in Epsom. You ask why it's called the bookies when it says Turf Accountant on the door, but she doesn't answer.

You tuck your rolled up towel under your arm and set off on the long walk to the beach. You can smell the sea before you see it. It smells of salt. Your swimsuit is blue, your favourite colour. It used to belong to your big sister, but it's too small for her now. You have worn your swimsuit under your clothes. It's better than getting undressed under a towel. The boys don't mind showing off their bums, but none of the girls want to be seen with no knickers. Karan Regan's mum has made her a towelling tent, with a hole for her head, so she can get changed under it. You ask if you can borrow it later, and she says yes.

The sea is a long way away. You keep your flip-flops on as you tiptoe over the pebbles, and then leave them far enough away, so that they don't get swept away by the waves. Last year, Sean Leahy threw your flip-flops in the sea, and you had to go home barefoot, as it was your fault. You were supposed to be keeping an eye on him, and you shouldn't have let him be so naughty. You thought it wasn't fair, like the time you found a ten bob note at the funfair, and you had to share it with your sisters.

You scream as you run into the water. It's freezing and it stings against your legs. The boys start splashing you. They are daring you to put your head under. It's best to get it over with; get goose pimples all over, rather than have your legs go numb while your chest and arms quiver like the jellyfish that stung you at Bognor that time. You need the loo, so you wee in the sea. Everyone else does it.

One time Christopher Langton did worse than that and told everyone, and you all said 'Eurgh.'

You get dried under Karan Regan's towelling tent. It's still damp after she has used it, but you slip your own towel underneath to dry yourself properly.

Mum has a shopping trolley full of food, and a damp flannel in a plastic bag. You eat your sandwiches and crisps, and then you have some ice cream, and Mum wipes your face with the damp flannel, rubbing hard, so it hurts. You blow up your crisp bag and pop it, then your little sister copies you like she always does, and you get annoyed. Your mum says she's only little and you have to make allowances.

You know it's the funfair next, and you're scared, because last year you went on the Wild Mouse on the roof of the arcade. You were in the front of the car when it jerked to a halt before turning the corner. It hung over the edge of the roof and you thought that it would fall off, killing you all, and your mums would be sad, but pleased that you all had clean faces and clean underwear on when the ambulance came.

You head back to meet the dads at the club. There is a slap up tea. You ask a lady if you are allowed to have another cake and she says you can have as many as you like, and you do, even though you feel sick by the end of it. Your shoulders are stinging and Karan Regan's nose is glowing like Rudolph's. Your brother's arms are bright red, as he is ginger and he burns easily. Tomorrow he will look like a lobster, covered with a pink crusty shell, when Mum puts the calamine lotion on him.

You get back on the coach. It's the first day of the football season, and you listen to the results on the radio to see how Chelsea has done. They won the cup this year and you skipped round the playground, arm in arm with Karan Regan and Sharon Corr, singing, "Chelsea 2, Leeds 1, alleluia."

You eat some rock, sucking hard, so that the pink disappears leaving a long white bullet with the letters all long and funny. Then you start on the giant sugar dummy. You are far enough away from Mum to escape the damp flannel until you get off the coach. Then it's into the Comrades Club for 'one last drink', that never is just one drink.

The mums aren't allowed to go to the bar, so the dads buy the drinks: beer, or Guinness for the dads and Dubonnet and lemonade, or a Cinzano for the mums. Coke for you, drunk through a striped paper straw out of a glass bottle. You run your fingers over the place where the words Coca-Cola are raised up on the glass. You like the way it feels.

You fall asleep across a couple of chairs, and somehow wake up in your own bed the next morning. Your hair is still in its ponytail, solid, sticking together from the salt. You know it's going to hurt when Mum pulls off the elastic band, and that the salt will be 'hell to get out' when she washes it, so you stay in bed as long as you can until you're hungry and you can smell bacon and you go downstairs.

A Tea Party

The baby smells of the milk that Mum leaves on the windowsill to go sour for making scones. Mum takes the nappy to the bucket in the bathroom, scrapes the poo into the toilet with a knife then sticks it in to soak. Sometimes I stir the nappies around with the big wooden tongs that Mum uses to lift the washing from the twin tub. Deeter Doh-er, Deeter Doh-er, clunking and chunking, Deeter Doh-er, then she lifts the steaming nappies into the sink to rinse off the bubbles, and then into the spin drier. It starts slow then screeches faster and faster, like a rocket ship taking off, and the twin tub dances across the floor, clunk-a, clunk-a. Mum lifts the lid and the clothes are pinned to the side like the people on that ride when the funfair came to Epsom Downs. They're turning slower now. I want to put my hand in and feel what the clothes are feeling, dizzy, but I mustn't stick my fingers in or I'll end up like that man in the corner shop who has a finger that stops halfway. We must pray for him, like when I prayed to get a kitten. Praying doesn't always get what you want, but you have to do it just in case, or horrible things might happen, like dying with a sin on your soul. That's why babies have to be baptised, to get rid of Original Sin. The priest washes it off with holy water. It's like washing poo off the nappies, except you can't put a baby in the washing machine, so the priest has to do it. He makes the sign of the cross on the baby's forehead with his thumb. That puts God in. God is in the priest's thumb.

Babies can't swim, so they only have the water on their head. I can nearly swim. I've been going to Epsom Baths with the school. We walk there in a crocodile, two by two, holding hands, and I'm always paired with Susan Saunders. There are four Susans in my class and five Catherines, but they are all called something different: two Cathys, One Kate, one Katie and a Catherine.

Uncle Michael doesn't live with us any more, now the new baby is here, as there isn't room. He's in digs now. Digs is where a lady cooks you breakfast and dinner, but you're not allowed to watch telly with her, only go in the kitchen for meals, and you have to pay her so much a week, and you get a bedroom. Sometimes all to yourself and sometimes with other men who might be friends or you might not even know them. Uncle Michael doesn't like it in digs. He meets Dad in the White Horse after work, and they stay there all evening, so he doesn't have to go back too early. Dad hardly ever comes home for his dinner these days; he goes straight to the pub. He doesn't say prayers with us either, as he's not there at bedtime, though sometimes he does and he brings back crisps and lemonade from the White Horse and bars of Cadbury's Dairy Milk that Charlie keeps behind the bar for when we play in the pub garden. There's something in the 'Our Father' about crisps: *give us our crisps as we forgive them that trespass against us*. It's the prayer that makes our father give us crisps, so Maggie and me keep saying it, even though Dad isn't there to help us.

Sometimes I wait and wait for Dad's donkey jacket to be on its hook in the hall and it's not there when I go to bed, and it's not there when I get up in the morning 'cause he's already gone to work.

Uncle Michael was funny when he first came over – that's what they call it when someone comes on the boat from Ireland, coming over. He came back with us when we'd been 'home' on holiday – that's what Mum calls it, going home. His mouth was hanging open when we got off the train at Euston, and he was staring. You don't get that many people in one place where he lived, in Ennistymon. Mum told him to stop catching flies, and did he want people to think he was bog Irish? Some people think Irish people aren't very clever, and you mustn't give them any ammunition.

He used to say hello to everyone in the street, like they do in Ireland, but Mum told him people don't do that in England, and he'd end up in Long Grove, which is the loony bin where she used to work before having us.

Uncle Michael gave me a tea set for my birthday. It has pink and blue flowers on it. There are little slots in the cardboard box for the saucers, and they stand upright, but slanting forwards, and there are round holes to put the cups in. There aren't any spoons. It's the best present I've ever had, but I didn't get to keep it nice for long. I got called to dinner, and left the tea set on the floor, and Brendan broke a cup. He cried, as he'd cut his finger on a sharp bit, then I cried when I saw what he'd done, and Mum got cross and told me to stop making such a racket as I'd set the baby off, and didn't she have enough to worry about without an old teacup. It wasn't old at all. Brendan didn't even get smacked, as he's only two, and I have to make allowances for him. I had a pain in my tummy when Mum threw the broken bits in the bin. I hate Brendan. I pinched him hard when no one was looking, then Mum got cross with him when he cried too long and set the baby off again. Crying just makes grown-ups angry; it never seems to be all right to cry.

I have tea parties with Maggie, and sometimes with Sindy and my teddies. I pretend to be Mum, and Maggie is Auntie Joan, and we talk like they do when Mum gets the Maxwell House out of the cupboard: about the other mums and aunties, and what Dr Evans has to say about Auntie Joan's trouble downstairs. I don't always understand what they're talking about, but if I ask I get sent out to play. I like listening to grown-up ladies, and seeing their bosoms when they've got babies with them. Bosom is a funny word. It sounds like it feels, all squashy and soft and smelling of talcum powder, like Mum's. The baby sucks it, and I get to see it when it's just us, or Auntie Pam and Auntie Joan, but not when Dad's around, or Uncle Bill or Uncle Dave. Men don't get to see bosoms, only ladies, children and babies.

Auntie Pam has a baby, but Auntie Joan doesn't have any, even though she's married. You can't have babies until you get married, God doesn't let you. Some people have lots of babies, and some have none at all, even though they like them a lot. I don't know why God won't let Auntie Joan have a baby. She holds Brendan really tight sometimes, and cuddles the new baby. Mum doesn't look very happy if she holds them for too long.

Mum doesn't cuddle me much these days; she's too busy. Auntie Joan doesn't cuddle me either – she prefers boys and tiny babies. I like girls best 'cause they don't break things. On the night the lady brought the baby, the fat lady with the clock on her bosom, Maggie and me were arguing about whether she'd brought a boy or a girl. She looked like a shadow puppet, standing in the doorway of our bedroom with the hall light behind her, and she told us to be quiet 'cause Mum was resting. Auntie Joan came in the morning and she asked the fat lady what kind of baby it was, and she said a girl, and Auntie Joan said, 'Never mind.' Auntie Joan did the ironing when Mum was resting. She held Brendan's shorts up to her face, and smelled them and rubbed them against her cheek. Her eyes were red, and her face looked like a scrunched-up paper bag.

When Maggie had her first Holy Communion, she had a new white dress with a skirt underneath made of scratchy stuff to make the dress stick out. The dress was silky with sewing on it, so you could feel the flowers and leaves that are stitched onto it. I closed my eyes and traced the flowers with my fingertips. I had to wash my hands first.

She had a hair band with pretend pink flowers on it, and white hairgrips to hold the veil in place. Mum said the outfit cost a fortune, but it will do for me when I have my first Holy Communion. Uncle Michael gave Maggie a white prayer book, but it's not as good as the tea set he gave me. A prayer book is only for one person – it's not for sharing – and you can't play with a prayer book.

I wore one of Maggie's old dresses, the one with stamps from all over the world printed on it. Dad prodded my tummy and said I looked like a parcel. I do like that dress, but it would have been nice to have a new one. Brendan gets new clothes all the time 'cause Kieran's clothes are too big to hand down, and Auntie Joan buys him bits and bobs too.

I held Dad's hand as we walked down the aisle, and I sat next to him, just me, as he was at the end of the row. He was wearing a suit, light grey, and a maroon tie that Mum had chosen at Burton's. Mum said that he couldn't go to a first Holy Communion in his work clothes, looking like he'd been dressed from the ragbag.

He'd been moaning about the baby before we left, saying couldn't Mum shut her up. Mum said he was keen enough to make them, but didn't want to know afterwards. He went quiet and they were staring at each other, him standing at the door, her at the sink, then Maggie walked into the kitchen in her dress and his face went soft again, and Brendan went charging at her, clinging onto her legs. It was like when you're waiting for a train and the gap between the platforms makes you feel dizzy, then trains come from different directions, and when they stop, the space doesn't feel so scary; you're just caught up in the excitement of where you're going.

The day of Maggie's first Holy Communion was the first time I'd seen Dad all week. The Sunday before, I'd had him all to myself at 11 o'clock Mass, as Maggie and Kieran had been to the 8 o'clock, and Brendan was playing up so he stayed home with Mum and the baby. The leaves were piled up in the park on the way to church, and Dad lifted me high so that I could kick the top of the hills of leaves and feel like I was walking on them, like when

Jesus walked on water. Mum doesn't let me kick the leaves in my good shoes; I'm surprised she lets me walk in them at all.

After Mass he took me to Stebbings. I chose a pink sugar mouse and he said not to tell the others, it's our secret. I sucked the sugar until all that was left was the string tail, and then Dad wiped my mouth with his hankie.

Mrs Roberts caught up with us – she had been to the 11 o'clock too. We walked her home, even though it was out of our way. She laughed every time Dad spoke, like she'd heard a funny joke.

'You'll come in for a cuppa and a slice of cake,' she said as we reached her gate. She offered me Victoria sponge, fondant fancies and iced fairy cakes with little silver balls on top. Her long red fingernails curled round the plate as she held it out to me, and as she leant over I could see the line where her bosoms met. I chose a fairy cake, but the silver balls were too hard to crunch, so I spat them out onto the plate. There was no silver then, just white.

She let me play tea parties with her big teapot and cups and saucers: her best china. She said I could play with what I liked as long as I didn't tell anyone that we'd been there. 'Is it a deal?' she said; I couldn't speak because I had cake in my mouth.

Dad and Mrs Roberts went away to talk about grown-up things. It was a bit funny as men and ladies don't usually talk together; the men talk to the men and the ladies talk to the ladies, especially after they get married. I think they talk and hold hands before they get married, but all that stops after they get babies.

Mrs Roberts came back into the kitchen, smiling with her bright red lips. She looked at me and laughed. 'We can't send you home like that,' she said, and she wiped my face with a tea towel, her face close to mine. Her mouth is too red. I can see it when I close my eyes. It's like the felt pen that Brendan got on the living room carpet that wouldn't come out.

Auntie Pam said something that Mum didn't like. She said that you shouldn't refuse your husband, as 'they seem to need it more than we do and they'll go elsewhere if they don't get it from us.' I think it's because Dad didn't come home for his dinner yesterday. Mum left his plate on top of a saucepan of hot water with another plate on top, upside down; it looked like a flying saucer. No donkey jacket in the hall at bedtime, and lamb chops, mashed potatoes, gravy and peas, all thick and gooey, scraped into the bin. Today, Mum didn't make him dinner. He could have gone to Uncle Michael's digs to eat, I suppose, but I don't think Mum likes the idea of another lady cooking for Dad.

I was woken up by voices and banging. Mum said, 'There's no point talking to you when you're three sheets to the wind,' and I couldn't understand what Dad said. I climbed into bed with Maggie and cuddled to her back. Then the baby started crying. Dad said something about the bloody baby, and then it sounded like something was knocked over, and Mum said, 'Eejit, you'll wake up all the children,' and he said, 'There's no peace in this house since that baby.' His voice sounded like Maggie's talking doll when the battery ran out.

I wanted to tell Maggie that I had cake at Mrs Roberts's, but I couldn't because it's a secret, and anyway she was tied up with her precious prayer book. So I took out the tea set and sat Sindy, Big Ted and Little Ted on the floor. I pretended to pour from the teapot, and I used the spare saucer to serve up cake. I made Victoria sponge and fondant fancies out of plasticine, though I couldn't get the colour right, as it had all been rolled into one brown ball.

'Will you have a cup of tea, Jack?' Sindy said. She leaned over so Big Ted could see where I'd pulled down her top to show the line where her bosoms meet. 'And some orange squash for the little one.' She poured a drink for little Ted. 'Would you like Victoria sponge, fondant fancies or iced fairy cakes with little silver balls on top?' Little Ted took a fairy cake. 'And now we must go and talk about grown-up things. Come on Jack.'

'Thank you, Mrs Roberts,' Big Ted said. I lifted Sindy and Big Ted onto the bed. Little Ted dropped his fairy cake on the carpet.

Mum stood in the doorway with the baby on her hip. She didn't say anything; she just stood there.

Later, she cooked Birds Eye Cod in Batter, boiled potatoes, peas and carrots. She made a flying saucer with Dad's dinner plate, and set it on a pan of water. She didn't do the washing-up; she slid down in an armchair in front of the telly. We watched *Coronation Street*, then *World in Action*, and it was only when Brendan fell asleep on the floor that she remembered to send us to bed. I said the 'Our Father' with Maggie, and I prayed in my head that Dad would come home for his Birds Eye Cod in Batter, and not go to another lady's house for dinner. I lay in bed until I heard the click of his key and his boot against the door; it sticks unless you push it hard. I heard his footsteps in the hall, and waited for Mum to say something, but all was quiet except for his breathing as he passed our bedroom door.

There was a pub smell on the stairs. I trod carefully, missing the creaky step, and stood by the living room door, which was almost shut. I pressed my face to the gap. There was a black and white film on the telly; a lady and a man were kissing. Mum was staring at the fire; the coal had gone grey with tiny bits of orange trying to shine through.

Cold Salt Water

He comes in with his shirt splattered with blood, and I say, 'Honest to God, Kieran.'

'Don't fuss, Mum,' he says like it's nothing to walk in the house with your nose spread across your face.

'What in Jesus' name happened?' No answer. 'Who were you with?'

'John and Chris.'

'And are they hurt too?'

'Leave it, Mum.'

I put my hand up to his face, but he dips from it. 'It's a rough old place, that dancehall. Tiffany's was it?'

'It's a disco, Mum, not a dancehall.'

And then his father's in the doorway, and I say, 'Will you look at the state of Kieran?' But he's three sheets to the wind himself, so I send him off to bed.

Well, I try to whip the shirt off the boy, but he holds it close around him. So I get a bucket ready: cold water with a good dash of salt. 'Come on now, Kieran,' I say, 'Let's have that shirt.' It's one of his good ones, a Ben Sherman. He unbuttons it. There are bruises like footprints on his chest.

'Did you get a look at them? Could you describe them to the police?'

'Please, Mum. It doesn't matter.'

'You've bruises all over!'

He flinches as I touch him. I can see that he's trying to hold on to the tears. I know the wobble in that lip, like when his father used to tell him that boys don't cry, so he'd sniff the snot back up into his nose, and pretend he was all right. But a mother knows. But a mother only knows by rummaging in his chest of drawers when he's out, through the piles of pennies and silver in the top drawer from his turned out pockets. I go in there when I'm short of money for the milkman, or need a 50p when the electric's gone. He doesn't like the rattle of the coins in his pockets, and how they spoil the line of his trousers. So they pyramid higher in the drawer, silver on copper, and slip like the coal in the bunker as the drawer opens, heavier each time I pull it out. And that's where I found that thing once – a rubber johnny, from a packet of three, and only the one left. I told him what Fr Westland would say. He just laughed. Though there have been times when I've thought, wouldn't we have been glad of one?

He's been worse since he's been working, acting like he's man of the house. Home at six, he slams the back door open against the kitchen dresser – there's a hole in the hardboard now – then he shouts, 'Where's my dinner?' When he was small, I could slap him across the back of the legs, but now he stands above me. I need to stand on a chair to look him in the eye.

'I'm off to bed,' Kieran says. I watch as he climbs the stairs, every step an effort. Whether he sleeps or not, I don't know, but I lie awake next to his snoring father. Every time I close my eyes, I can't stop seeing the footprints on my boy's chest.

In the morning, he's so stiff he can hardly raise an arm, so I knock at Mick Bennett's house, and ask would he tell them at the factory that Kieran won't be in. Then I run Kieran a hot bath to see would it ease him a little, and make him egg and bacon when he's out and dressed. Although it hurts to see him like that, it's nice, in a way, to have my boy to myself, with Jack and the children off for the day.

I've the radio on in the kitchen, and the news headlines come over, of the latest from the IRA, a pub in Guildford, not ten miles up the road. I know there'll be hard stares when I ask for the veg at the greengrocer, when I open my mouth to speak, as if it was me that laid that bomb. 'Are you ready to tell me?' I say, as he wipes the yolk of his egg off the plate with a half-bitten slice of fried bread. He holds up his mug, and I pour some more tea. 'Shall we go to the police?' He half-drains the mug, then slams it down on the table. The tea splashes up the sides then settles again. 'Or was it you that started it? I know your temper.'

The full story of the bombing comes on the radio. 'Switch it off,' he says.

'God knows why your father stands up for that lot,' I say, 'it doesn't do us any good, those of us that have to live here.' He stares at his plate, his fingertips pressing into the edge of the table. 'Is that what the fight was over?' I say.

'It's nothing to do with me, what the Irish get up to,' he says, 'I ain't Irish.'

I wipe my hands on a tea towel and turn to him. 'Only every ounce of blood that flows through your veins.'

'It don't make me Irish.' He butters a slice of bread. I can see how it's bothering him to eat, with his top lip split. Part of me wants to slap him, and the rest of me wants to cradle him. I picture him lying on the ground as the heavy boots hit his chest. And I think of how he's stopped going to the Tara club, how it's Tiffany's on a Saturday night, out with his packet of three: Durex, approved to British standards.

I go to the bucket where I'd steeped the shirt the night before. The water is pink, the blood seeping into the crystals. I drain the bucket into the sink, rinse the shirt, then run more cold water into the bucket, emptying the remainder of the packet of Saxa into it. I watch the shirt sink, pushing it down so it's covered.

More Katharine than Audrey

ome Dancing is on Tuesday. Some lose track, but it's mince and potatoes on Monday, *Come Dancing* on Tuesday, sheets changed Wednesday and so on. I'm not supposed to watch it – the lights go off at nine – but I turn the volume low so the staff won't hear. I close my eyes and I dance around the room, then I'm in the black taffeta, and the skirt and my hips are swinging. If the nurses catch me, when they're doing their rounds, their eyes smile above the masks. The flickering of the screen reflects on the walls. My room is a dancehall.

Mrs Davies left the ward today. There are two of us left, so it won't be long until it's my turn. I asked Rankin how far it is to London on the train. It takes half an hour, she said; half an hour from Epsom to Waterloo, and a little longer to Victoria. It seemed to take as long as that to walk the corridors when I first came here. Windows either side, so I could see the grounds and the buildings with the other wards, the laundry and the kitchens. The kitchens are a long way off: sometimes there's porridge, sometimes cornflakes, but always tea and toast, and the toast is cold.

I have my own telly, now that most of the others have gone. There are films in the afternoon: Humphrey Bogart and Katharine Hepburn in *The African Queen*, she as ugly as me, and a film star. It was the other Hepburn, Audrey, that I would have liked to be: petite and pretty, like a fairy gone to live in the world of men. She was a nurse in *The Nun's Story*, tempted by a handsome doctor in a hospital in the Congo; Peter Finch played the doctor. She didn't succumb, but she wasn't for the convent in the end. 'You are a worldly nun' the Reverend Mother said, or was it the Mother Superior? The times I saw that film, and each time the tightness in my chest, a hankie at the ready when she goes into that room at the end of the film, to leave the convent, and she gets her old clothes back, the ones she came in with, and there's no one there to say goodbye, as if it's a disgrace, wanting to go back into the world.

I could never be like Audrey Hepburn; my hips are too wide.

We had the cowboys back in Mitchelstown – Randolph Scott, Gary Cooper, John Wayne; he was a favourite of Molly's. And I loved Jimmy Stewart. They have them on the telly, too, and it's as if I'm in the middle rows of the picture house with Molly.

I'm like Audrey Hepburn after all, a worldly woman kept apart from the world. She got sick in that film: tuberculosis was it? She was isolated in a beautiful treehouse, given the 'gold cure' and tended to by Peter Finch. And here's me in Long Grove with Rosina Bryars and the nurses. No gold cure for me. No Peter Finch. But it won't be long before they find the right combination of drugs for me, as they did for the others.

Pea soup it said in the books: *six to eight motions a day, and it looks like pea soup*. That's just how it was when I had the fever. I can't eat it to this day: that and rhubarb. Mammy used to boil it up to clean the pans; I worried it would strip the lining of my stomach.

Rankin cut me some roses on Sunday. She brought red and white, but a nurse will always arrange them separately, or there will be blood and bandages before the day's out, so the white went to Rosina and I have the red. They were in bud, so they'd last longer. I've been watching them unfurl. They smell like summer, like the outdoors as I remember it. When the petals drop onto the bedside table, I want them left there to darken, then brown. I want the leaves left to wither on the stem, to watch them shrivel; but the cleaner comes in every day, gloved, overalled, and changes the water, wipes the fallen from the bedside table with a cloth dipped in disinfectant, and it masks the scent of the roses.

I close my eyes, and I see the roses in the garden blossom, fade and drop. I walk on a carpet of withered petals, and pinch them between my toes. Then I'm in the field back home with Molly, and we're running fast towards the sun.

Rosina isn't up to much now; she'd as soon eat a rose as smell it.

I was used to the smell of disinfectant when I was nursing, and the way it changes colour in the bucket when you add water. Sid offered me Pernod once, added a dash of water. It clouded in the glass like disinfectant; smelled of the aniseed balls that they tipped into paper bags from the teardrop-shaped bowl of the scales in the sweetshop in Mitchelstown. Disinfectant would do it, if I could get hold of some; I could mix it with the water in my bedside glass and pretend it was Pernod.

There's no wildness in these gardens, just straight lines and fresh mown and leaves piled up in the autumn. Nothing like the fields back home with the brambles and crab apples. Off we'd go: Molly and me, with bowls to fill, and our arms and our clothes would be torn and purple-bruised with juice. The sweetest would always be the furthest in, and didn't we always want the sweetest, the juiciest, to reach for the best, not to settle?

The first time I offered a brimming bowl to Da, I was so small I had to raise it to reach his hands, hanging like shovel-ends from his arms. He said No; he wouldn't touch those things, full of spiders and flies. I never offered them again. I gave them up to Mammy for the crumble. His was made separate with crab apples and lots of sugar. He didn't like the black stain on the apples' flesh.

Da thought it was the boys I was after when I went to England. Jesus, with what I've seen of men's parts, what's there to get excited about? Like snails tucked in a hood, and sometimes, sick as they were, it would rear up at the feel of the sponge. God, the first time I saw one at full length I called for Sister. I thought something awful had happened. Shrub came running at my shrieks, and when she saw what had alarmed me, she pursed her lips to stop the giggles. Sister said, 'I think Mr Ericson is well enough to wash himself.' Shrub dragged me into the sluice room and collapsed, tears rolling down her cheeks. Oh, she took me off something rotten: *Sister, come quick it's Mr Ericson's...* I couldn't even find a word to describe it at the time. And we were both in stitches, with her attempt at my accent.

It was last names, even off duty. It was Shrub, Gates, McCallion, and so on. You'd say, 'Is Shrub on tonight?' or, 'I've the same shifts as McCallion.' Then the crowd I went round with called me Josie, as there was another Noreen. I forgot I was Noreen at all until I came here; it was in my notes, and that's what they go by. I still think of her as Shrub, though she'd a beautiful Christian name – Annette. But that's how it was, and that's how I remember.

You didn't have to choose what to wear, to be as good as, to have a style. You just wore the uniform, maybe dressed with a frilled cuff if Sister would allow. Rankin wears a cuff and a fob-watch like I had, pinned to the chest. I can see it through the plastic apron. She's my favourite, Rankin; she listens, really listens. Some of them just talk to each other. I suppose we did, too, me and Shrub: tipped the patients forward like they were one of the pillows we were tidying, eased them back, talking over them the whole time. As long as the ward was spick and span, that's what Sister was after.

The fool I was, falling for a woman. I'd study Shrub's lips, the soft hairs on the nape of her neck below her pinned-up hair when she was on the ward, the curl of her hair when it was down, when we went dancing or to the pictures. She hadn't a notion that I dreamed of her, dreams from which I woke with the sheets twisted, dreams of parting her lips with mine, her face cupped in my hands, of slipping a satin nightdress from her shoulders, like the ones they wear in the films, watching it fall to the floor. Sometimes, on the ward, she'd brush against my bosom in passing, and the heat of those dreams would flush my face and neck.

When I first arrived at Euston station from the boat train, no one smiled or allowed me to catch their eye; no one said hello. It was just after the war – we weren't involved, in Ireland, so I'd no experience of what they'd been through. Nice enough people, but there was this reserve, and not just because I was Irish. It was as if they'd had something removed, like patients recovering from an operation, trying to get back to normal, but no longer sure what normal felt like. But the nurses, there was a spark in them; they knew how to dance, to drink, to let go. You never knew what you'd encounter on the next shift: a motorbike accident; a patient with a tumour; a family gathered to hear bad news about their father; and the bedpans and bottles, everything scrubbed and sterilised. So it was living for the moment.

There weren't always men to dance with, so the women danced together, and if there were any men, the women would flutter round them like moths to an old suit. A man could have a different woman for each dance. I wasn't bothered; if a man asked, I'd dance with him, but I was happiest with Shrub.

So when I went home to Mitchelstown I was full of stories, of the hospital and the friends and the dancing. Mammy clapped her hands and wrung them in turn. She was in envy of me, for getting away and making something of myself; but another part of her was afraid I'd go to the bad. She was wearing her thousand-times-washed dress with the faded paisley swirls of pink and mauve, the lace of her slip peeking out from the hem, and there I was talking of taffeta and satin and the new coat I'd bought for the winter. As for Da, he was all hard edges, and as broad as he was tall, with no softening at my touch or my words.

I tapped a cigarette from the packet, and tried to light it with the matches from my coat pocket. It had rained on the walk from the bus stop in town, and they were damp, so I put a spill into the embers of the fire. It was as if I'd stripped naked and danced on the table, the blustering and the language from Da, how I'd been ruined by England and nursing. How I was setting a bad example to my sister Molly. I wasn't to smoke either in or out of the house. And when I laid in late he said, 'There's no holiday here, my girl,' expecting me to go back to my old chores.

I went to a dance at the Mayflower with some of the old crowd, and Jimmy O'Gorman walked me home. He'd been disappointed by a girl he liked; she was dancing with another boy the whole evening. We were great friends, Jimmy and me, and I linked arms with him on the way up the hill. He'd had a drink, and it was as much me holding him up as him walking me home. We parted at the fork in the road below the house.

Da was waiting at the gate, late as it was. 'Are the men in England not enough for ye?' He slapped me round the head. I reeled, but I stood my ground.

'It's only Jimmy. He walked me home.'

'Walking, is it, with everything on show?' We'd had words about how I was dressed before I left the house. I'd wrapped a stole around me to placate him, pinned it with a brooch, but I'd whipped it off at the dancehall. He went for my head again, but I ducked from his open palm. He slapped me round the back of the thighs as he had when I was a child. 'There'll be a different fella every night in London, the hoor you are.'

I flung my head back, the offending bosom thrust forward. I picked up the yard broom and held it in front of me; handle up, to hit him should he come at me again. But Mammy ran out and bundled me inside with Molly. I could hear his old clichés: *no daughter of mine*, and the like. They wouldn't find house room in a decent film script. And I was as bad, battering against the bedroom door with my fists, rattling the handle to get out.

'Mammy locks the door when he has a temper,' Molly said. She looked so small in her nightdress. Her hair hung in waves, released from the plaits they were tied in by day. I came away from the door and sat next to her on the bed. My hands shook as Molly took hold of them. 'Da says I'm not to go to England, but as soon as I've finished school I'll be away. I want to go to the dances, have all the lovely clothes.' Her hand dropped to my dress, and she rubbed the fabric of the hem between her fingers and thumb. I undressed and got into the bed with her.

'It wasn't so bad when you were here,' she said. 'Could you stay, do you think, until I'm ready to go with you?' I didn't answer. I stroked her hair until she fell asleep, as I used to when we'd shared the bed before I left for England. I lay awake until I heard Mammy making the breakfast for Da, heard him leave for the fields, and heard the turn of the key in the bedroom door, and Mammy going out to draw water from the well.

I slipped from beneath the curve of Molly's arm, gathered my clothes and left. Why would I stay and be beaten and called a whore? Or end up like Mammy, chopping the vegetables, cutting the meat for the stockpot, sweeping the floor, taking out the ashes and sitting on the doorstep waiting for a passing neighbour to bring a bit of gossip.

I sent money home, as was expected, and Mammy wrote letters, begging me to make my peace with Da. I didn't write back, just sent the money. When I came here there was no more money to send.

You'd think, with her being a nurse that she'd know, but they're as prone to such foolishness as anyone, and Annette Shrub fell for a baby. She asked me what should she do, about being in trouble. I said what Mammy would have said: she should get the man to do the right thing.

She asked if I'd be her maid of honour, but I said 'Can you see me in a froth of a dress with these lumbering hips?' Truth is, I couldn't face the wedding at all. I prayed that that her husband-to-be would have a terrible accident and there would be a funeral, not a wedding. Then I hoped that I would break a leg, so I couldn't walk into the church; but the day came and the fella and me were both intact, so the ceremony went ahead. I sat in the front row and stared at her soft neck through the stiffness of her veil. Thinking I might get the chance should her hair become unpinned, and I could caress the stray strands into place, a hair grip in my mouth, press her hair to the back of her head for a second while I reached for the grip. But all went off as planned, not a hair or a word out of place, and Shrub became Mrs Someone-else.

Paper and pen, pen and paper: I ask for them when Rankin brings my dinner – fish pie, as it's Friday – and I start to write home. Someone in the town will know Molly, will recognise the name, even though she might be married now. Someone will know where she lives if she's left Mitchelstown. I keep the letter short, just telling Molly where I am and asking would she like to get in touch, and I ask Rankin to post it. It might take Molly a month or two to write back after a shock like that, a letter after so long.

My hair was good, thick and wavy and almost black, and there was never a problem with my skin. Just those lumbering hips and the bosoms I didn't know what to do with. Cover them up, Mammy would say, though the devil in me said show off your assets. The men had a fair love of them. When I wore the black taffeta with the red roses and a glimpse of cleavage – a glimpse was all they needed – some of them couldn't keep their eyes away as they asked for a dance. I wanted to tilt their chins with the heel of my hand, so their eyes would be level with mine. How they'd have loved to get their hands on my chest. It wasn't *their* hands I wanted.

Annette gave me a photo: bride and groom, beauty and the beast. I cried over it every night until I could bear it no more. I burned it in the sink, watched the faces blacken and curl, and then rinsed the ashes down the plughole.

Shrub gave up on the dancing, so I went with McCallion instead. I wore the black taffeta with roses again that night, black stockings, heels, my hair up with a mother of pearl clip, and red lipstick to match the roses on the dress. This man came over, and it was me he was interested in, not McCallion, though she was the slimmer and prettier of the two of us. I danced with him, but it was Shrub I thought of: how I would tuck my hand close around her fingers as I swung her, pull her close, push her back, the lightest of touches as she twirled beneath my arm, her finger looped in my finger and thumb, and her skirt flying, her hair streaming behind her and the set of her mouth as she concentrated on the steps, and the click of her heels on the dance floor; the lightest of clicks – click-click – and the flush of her cheeks as we fell back to the table for our drinks.

He was kind, this man, Sid – older than me, well spoken; a proper English gentleman – and we fell into a courtship of sorts.

When I get out of here I'll take a flat in Tooting Bec, be close to things. I'll wander round the market with my basket in the morning, stop for a cup of tea and a slice of toast and jam at Luigi's cafe, maybe look up Shrub, if I can remember her last name (what was the name of that fella she married?). Or just sit in the café and wait for Godot. He took me, that Sid who courted me, took me to the theatre to see it. Hadn't a clue what it was about – two old tramps talking and waiting for a man that never turned up. I didn't get it. Much preferred a bit of a musical when I went to see a show, or to go for a meal and a swing round the dance floor.

I could do that, too: take a look at a dancehall in Kentish Town, go and watch the young ones, maybe show them a few moves myself! I'll need a new wardrobe. It won't be like Audrey Hepburn in *The Nun's Story*, they won't give me back the same clothes that I came in with. They'll have been incinerated. And decades out of fashion in any case. Any old rags, they give you here; the Lord only knows where they find them. But I keep up with the trends in the magazines that Rankin gives me after she's read them. I suppose she's not allowed to take them out of here anyhow, but it's good of her nonetheless.

The food came and it was grand: steak, fried, fancy potatoes done with cream and thin slices of onion, a little salad of lettuce and tomatoes and cucumber in a glass dish of its own at the side of the main plate, and cloth serviettes embossed with an ivy leaf motif. I dove in with my fork turned the wrong way. Sid smiled, turned it round in my hand and showed me how to push the peas onto the fork, to soak the gravy with a little potato on the prongs. He ate like a lady, little bites. And he stared at me, a shine in his pupils, but it was the food that got me going, not him. It was all I could do to stop lifting the plate and licking it clean. After Shrub married, I got so thin that my curves all but straightened, but my appetite returned that night. And a hand on my knee beneath the table, which did nothing for me, but I let him.

He took me dancing in Kentish Town, fingers pressing into my back in the slow dances, his cheek to mine, and his cigarette breath on my neck. We twirled round the hall, and my frock swirled and flicked, and he smiled.

That was the night he gave me Pernod. I wasn't much of

a drinker, in spite of what Da thought of me, and I warmed to Sid with the drink inside me. I placed a hand at his back as we walked from the taxi, leaned my head on his shoulder. He turned to kiss me. His moustache scratched at my top lip. It was cold, raining; we sneaked past his landlady's door. There were drips coming through the ceiling in the attic room, pots and pans laid out to catch them. He drew me onto the bed beside him, slipped the dress from my shoulders and kissed my neck. His face was red; he was breathless. I shouldn't have led him on, so.

That was the night that did for me: someone in the kitchen of that restaurant. Someone that was a typhoid carrier like I am now, not washing their hands, passing it on to all that ate there.

The daylight is fading. I have to wait for the lights to go on. I'm down to the last page of the *Daily Mail* with those pictures: men on the moon, looking like they're underwater in diving suits, and more men at Houston staring at screens, pencils dangling from their fingers like cigarettes.

If I had a suit like that I could go into town and shop for myself at Woolworth's instead of asking Rankin to get bits and bobs for me. I could get a cup of tea and a jam tart at a cafe. Last night I dreamt of cafes and pubs and shops and crowds, of sliding into a seat on the top deck of a bus, arms and thighs butted up against the woman in the window seat, carrier bags arranged around my feet. A bit of food from the International Stores, a pair of tights, a new blouse, a lipstick, tickets in my handbag for the stalls at the Odeon from the night before, a dab of perfume behind my ears.

I wouldn't be able to drink the tea, I suppose, in a spaceman's suit.

I asked for some knitting needles and wool, and I am clicking my way through a scarf, russet and green, to match the coat I have picked out from the *News of the World* magazine. I don't want to order it; I'll wait till I can try it on. I could try knitting gloves, but they're tricky.

Rankin brought me a box of Christmas cards. I've written one for Rosina, one for Rankin, some for the other nurses and for Mavis the cleaner. There's been no reply to the note I sent Molly in the summer. I'll try again, with a card. I choose a holy one with the blessed Virgin and the infant Jesus, haloes lighting their faces. I give it to Rankin to post.

A Day at the Races

The dishes were stacked floor to ceiling on open wooden shelves. 'These have to be washed,' Colin said, waving an arm in front of the piles of plates. 'They haven't been used since the last meeting.' Kaz and Jackie stared at the wall of crockery. 'Quick sharp,' Colin said, the races start tomorrow. Don't want our diners eating off dusty plates.' He handed Kaz a bottle of washing-up liquid and two tea towels before dashing out of the kitchen.

Jackie lifted a stack of plates and carried them over to the butler sink as Kaz filled it with soapy water. 'Bloody hell,' said Jackie, 'These are heavy.' She lifted the first plate to hand to Kaz. The plate beneath was covered in a congealed mess that had once been food, with tinges of grey mould. The next plate was the same, and the one beneath.

'Bastards,' Kaz said. 'Fancy leaving the dishes like that. Must have been the last washer-uppers, back in August last year.'

'Dirty bastards,' Jackie said.

'Dirty lazy bastards,' Kaz said.

Jackie thought, for a moment, of leaving the dishes there, of walking out, or at least of finding Colin to complain, but she had no idea how or where to find him. He had met them at the entrance to the Grandstand that morning, rushed them through the building, up staircases, through bars and dining rooms to their kitchen, then rushed off again. He seemed like the kind of person that never stopped. She had visions of catching a glimpse of him as he flitted from one room to another, then never seeing him again. Might as well get on with it. There would be money at the end of the week, to buy records or clothes, or to save a bit towards her holiday.

By lunchtime, only the lowest length of shelving was clear. The shelves themselves were dusty and cobwebbed, but they hadn't been told to wipe those down, so they left them as they were. If only they knew where their food was coming from – the posh nobs with their top hats and fancy clothes – the dusty kitchens used for only two weeks out of fifty-two, when you added up the days. The rest of the year, the kitchens, restaurants and bars were left to the mice.

Colin came into the kitchen at half-past twelve. 'You'll have to work faster than that,' he said, casting a critical eye over the girls' work. They stood open-mouthed, but before they had a chance to speak he was whizzing out the door. 'Lunch break', he said. 'Come down to the marquee out on the grass. There's a meal for you.'

It was some kind of stew, meat with a thin gravy, not like the Bisto-thickened kind that Jackie's mum made at home. She picked out a green leaf and held it up. 'Look, this must have dropped into the stew. Shall we say something?'

'Shh,' said Kaz. 'It's a bayleaf. I saw one once when my auntie took us to a posh meal in a hotel. You don't eat it; leave it on the side.'

There was no lunch break once the race meeting was underway. Not for the kitchen staff. They got the pickings from the plates cleared from the white-clothed tables in the restaurant. Leftovers from abandoned cheese boards, rounds of Bel Paese wrapped in foil, lumps of something stinky with green spots, served with Carr's Water Biscuits, which tasted like cardboard. If that was what the posh nobs ate, they could keep it. Jackie's favourite snack was a digestive biscuit, spread thick with butter, with a big lump of cheddar on top. Followed by a slice of apple pie.

Jackie's Mum made apple pies on a Sunday, while the roast was cooking. Enough pies to last into the week. The apples were stewed with tons of sugar, the pastry made with butter. Sugar in the pastry, too, and plenty sprinkled on top, once the pastry lid was spread over the apples, unwrapped from the rolling pin, from one side of the dish to the other. Jackie took care to cut three leaves out of pastry to go around the slit in the centre of the pie, to let the steam out. She would score veins on the leaves with a knife, then stick them down with a little bit of water.

Sunday was always the same, or it used to be before Jackie started going out with Jason. Mass first thing, then the rest of the morning in the kitchen with her mum, peeling spuds and carrots first, then the apples for the pies. Then dinner, and the washing up, which seemed to go on forever. It was pretty boring after that: the God Slot on the telly – *Stars on Sunday* – and then some costume drama. Homework had to be finished, too. She'd do that in the kitchen, listening to the radio while the charts counted down to Number One. But since she'd been seeing Jason, she went round his house after Sunday dinner, and stayed until 9.30, so she'd always be home for *That's Life*.

Jason was Kaz's big brother, five years older than Jackie. He worked as a clerk at the Labour Exchange in Epsom, and he owned a motorbike, which he rode on L-plates. He wasn't supposed to carry passengers, but sometimes Jackie rode pillion. She was afraid of how fast he rode, but when she told him this, he only sped up, so now she said nothing, just closed her eyes.

Jason loved Jackie's mum's apple pies. Her mum would serve him a big slice with a cup of tea whenever he came round. The fuss she made, you'd think he was her mum's boyfriend, not Jackie's. And he played up to it, praising the slice of pie to high heaven; flirting, almost. But her dad, he barely acknowledged Jason. He just gave a small nod and a sharp 'Hello'. It got so her mum made a small pie on a Sunday, which she kept just for Jason when he came round on a Tuesday. She never measured the ingredients, just seemed to know the right ratio of butter to flour to sugar. It didn't work so well when she made Victoria sponges, which were rather solid, not like the shop-bought ones at Kaz and Jason's house.

Another pile of crockery and cutlery arrived in the kitchen as the next race was called. The posh nobs had left their half-eaten plates, their barely-begun bottles of champagne, and hurried out to the terrace, binoculars slung around necks, to watch the horses hurtling round Tattenham Corner.

'More money than bleeding sense,' Mavis said, as she pushed through the swing-door with a third-full bottle of champagne. The waitresses had no time to stop and swig; the man they called, 'Yes Chef' with his white jacket and tall hat that puffed up like the hats the little men wore on the Homepride flour packets, he kept them busy.

'Two fish, one steak, one chicken,' he shouted. As if they were answering their names called on the school register, Mavis and Pam the waitresses shouted, 'Yes Chef,' and bustled out the door, plates in hands and balanced on their forearms. As the door swung open and back, Jackie could see the food placed on tables where no-one sat.

'Delivered, Table 5,' Pam said. 'No bugger there.' She winked at the girls.

'Let's swop,' Kaz said. She shook the water from her hands as she lifted them from the sink. Jackie wrung out the tea towel she'd been using, and passed the one on the rail to Kaz. She had hung it there earlier in a vain effort to dry it out; it was still wet through. At home, she'd have changed the dishwater by now. It was grey and there were no soap bubbles remaining. But there was little left of the washing-up liquid that had to last for the day.

Mavis had left the champagne bottle on the 'dirty' side of the sink, with the dishes waiting to be washed. There was a 'clean' table for those that had been dipped in the murky water and wiped with the sodden tea towel.

Cheers and groans arose from the terraces. The chatter of the punters could be heard once again from the other side of the door, and service resumed. Mavis and Pam brought in the untouched plates they'd delivered some minutes before, as new diners took their places at the tables. Kaz and Jackie tucked into the cooling sauté potatoes from the 'Two fish' plates, and scraped the rest of the food into the open bin. Kaz took a swig from the champagne bottle to wash it down. She grimaced. 'Can't see what all the fuss is about,' she said, before passing the bottle to Jackie. 'If this is what the top-hatted twats like, they can keep it.'

Jackie coughed as the bubbles fizzed in her throat. 'I'd rather have a lager and lime.'

Jackie saw less of Kaz and her other friends, now she had a boyfriend. And with Jason being twenty, he wasn't so interested in the places that fifteen-year-olds liked to go. It was nice to spend this time together, with Kaz. Even if they were up their elbows in dirty dishes.

The remains of a cheese board came through. Jackie tore off the pointed end of a wedge of cheese, which had blue lines running through it. It tasted as rank as it smelled, but she was dead hungry, and after she and Kaz had drained more champagne bottles that came through from the tables, she was feeling light-headed.

Eventually, the kitchen slowed. The last race had run, no more shouting from the terraces. Mavis and Pam and 'Yes Chef' cleaned down the preparation surfaces and the cooker hobs. 'Yes Chef' took off his hat and unbuttoned his white jacket, Mavis and Pam untied their frilled aprons. The hum of the kitchen quietened to a light clank of cleanish plate on cleanish plate, which Kaz and Jackie ferried in stacks to the shelves on the other side of the kitchen, ready for Day Two.

'You coming down the fun fair?' Kaz asked.
'Hmm, tempting, but I'm meeting Jason later. I need to

get changed.'

Kaz frowned. 'Aw, come on. Half an hour won't make much difference. Have a bit of fun.' She nudged Jackie's arm with her own. Jackie knew how angry Jason got if she was late, or if she wasn't dressed as he liked. He hadn't liked the sleeveless top she'd worn on their last date, and was grumpy all evening. She thought for a moment. If she had a wash instead of a bath … 'A cat's lick and a promise,' as her mum would say … then she could go to the fair with Kaz and still meet Jason on time.

The girls walked past a row of open-doored caravans, each with a head-scarved woman inside waiting to tell people's fortunes. Trade was slow in the gap between the races ending and the locals coming out for the evening. The funfair was not very crowded, either. The girls had an extra-long go on the Waltzer, with a long-haired guy spinning their car so much that Jackie had trouble walking in a straight line when she stepped off.

'Good to see you laughing,' Kaz said. 'You've been far too serious since you've been going out with my brother. Come on, let's go on the Big Wheel.' *See the Fair from the Air*, the sign said, as they climbed the steps. As they rose, Jackie caught sight of her French teacher, as the bar dropped onto his lap on the Octopus. There was a story at school that he was descended from French aristocracy. Although his name was Monsieur Villeneuve, he was known only as 'The Count'; even the other teachers used that name. At school, he regarded his pupils with disdain, looking down his noble French nose as if he really belonged in an ornate French chateau with a butler serving him drinks on a silver salver.

Today he was wearing a belted raincoat, like Inspector Clouseau, with a furled umbrella clamped between his knees, his hands resting on its handle, rather than the safety bar of the ride. He looked odd in that setting, out of place, as though he was sampling the rides as a social experiment, to see how the peasants spent their leisure time.

Epsom Downs lay beneath them as the car of the Big Wheel rose: the racetrack; the Grandstand where they had spent the day washing dirty dishes, drinking champagne and nibbling at chunks of cheese; the stalls where Jackie had wandered with her family at other race meetings. Everything on sale from Teasmades and crockery sets to cuddly toys, like a selection from the conveyor belt on *The Generation Game*. The men on the stalls would gather a crowd around them, calling out 'Ridiculous prices, today only.' The prices would diminish every few seconds: 'I'm not asking you fifteen pounds, not even ten. Five pounds the lot.' One punter would come forward, then a whole crowd of them, fivers in hand. Jackie's brother had bought a watch at the last race meeting. It stopped working after a week.

'Better get moving,' Jackie said as the ride ended and the bar was lifted.

'Oh, go on, just one more ride.'

'No, I'd better go.'

They walked back towards the Grandstand, where Jackie could catch a bus home from one side of the road and Kaz on the other, back past the row of open-doored caravans.

'Let's have our fortunes told,' Kaz said.

'Dunno. I'm not supposed to … Mum says it's dabbling with the occult.'

'Your mum isn't here, though, is she?' They stopped at a van with a big sign outside: *Gipsy Lee, Palmistry, Clairvoyance, Character Readings*. 'Come on, we'll go in together. It'll be fun.'

Gipsy Lee leaned over Kaz's hand and studied her palm. 'You have a long lifeline,' the woman said. 'But you see this break here? Your life will be broken – by illness, perhaps an accident.' She raised her head to look at Kaz. 'But you are strong and you have courage. You will overcome many difficulties.' Kaz nodded.

'Now, the other young lady.' Gipsy Lee held Jackie's palm. 'Your heart line tells me much. You love well, but you do not always love wisely.' She stared at the palm in silence for a while. 'You are young, my dear. You will have many lovers in your life. You must learn not to give your heart to those that don't deserve it.'

'Could have told you that myself,' Kaz said, as they stepped down from the caravan. 'Jason might be my brother, but I'll tell you this for nothing – no need to cross my palm with silver – you're too good for him.'

It was true that life was not free and easy with Jason. He liked things a certain way. He liked to choose what they did, how they spent their time together. It was because he was older, she guessed. He didn't have so much spare time as Jackie, with her being at school and him being at work, so he liked to plan things. The days they met were set – Tuesdays at her house, Friday and Saturday nights out, Sunday afternoons at his house, where they watched *Celebrity Squares* with his family and drank endless cups of tea.

At first, he'd taken her out: to the bowling alley, to the pictures, and once they had gone out with another couple (his age) to an Indian restaurant. She liked the way they mixed sweet things with savoury in Indian meals. She'd had pineapple with chicken, and lychees were her favourite. But now, there weren't so many 'dates' as such; just efforts to get her alone, and to get inside her knickers. On one date, they'd travelled up and down to London in a single train carriage. They hadn't got out at Waterloo, just stayed in the carriage and kissed. He'd unclipped her bra that day. She was worried that someone might get in at the next stop, and she wouldn't be able to do it up. But no-one did. He had wanted her to put her hand down his jeans, too, but she'd been too scared. She liked the kissing, the hand-holding. That was enough for her. But he was older and wanted more.

Once Jackie got home and collapsed on the sofa, she noticed how much her feet hurt, and how tired she was. Her hair and clothes stank of kitchen smells. All she really wanted to do was have some dinner and lie on her bed listening to the radio until she fell asleep.

'Your dad must have had a good day,' her mum said. 'He hasn't been home yet. Must have backed a winner.'

'Oh yes, the races,' Jackie said. 'Haven't seen a horse all day. All I saw was the kitchen sink and dirty dishes.'

'Poor love, you must be shattered. Still, think of the money.'

'That's why we're doing it.'

'Do you want some dinner? It won't be for another hour?'

'No time. I'm meeting Jason.'

'OK, I'll put some bits on a plate for you.'

Jackie quickly ate a sausage roll, a bit of salad and a crusty roll. She played a cassette, *Motown Chartbusters Volume 6*, as she got ready to go out. 'Just my Imagination' by The Temptations came on, her favourite slow dance song. She longed to dance to it with Jason, but Jason didn't dance, fast or slow. She missed dancing; between school, homework and seeing Jason, there were no spare evenings when she could go out to a disco. Plus Jason didn't like her going out without him.

They'd been to a Valentine's Day disco at Epsom College a few months before. A schoolfriend's brother went there. She'd got to dance with her friends that night, while Jason sat on the other side of the hall. At the end of the night, he'd said that he'd enjoyed it, going out together but being separate, just watching her amongst her friends. She thought it strange. He didn't really mix with other people at the party, just sat by the bar, watching.

She put on her pale grey trousers and a dark-blue long-sleeved T-shirt with a pale-blue star motif. Jason preferred her in a skirt, but trousers were better for going on the rides. Her hair could have done with a wash, but it would take too long to dry. She pulled on her satin bomber jacket as she said goodbye to her mum.

'Are you sure you'll be warm enough?' her mum said. 'It is only May, after all. It can get quite cool in the evenings.'

'I'll be fine, Mum. See you later.'

'Not too late. Don't forget you have work in the morning.'

In spite of her efforts Jackie was late. The bus didn't turn up. She could have walked, but her feet were so tired. And the next bus was running late, too. Always the same on race days. Delayed by heavy traffic earlier on, and they never seemed to catch up.

Jason was standing at the bus stop by the Berni Inn on Tattenham Corner. As Jackie descended from the platform of the 406, she saw The Count on the terrace of the pub, sipping from a glass of red wine. He saw her, too, and raised his glass in greeting. She waved back. This did not go unnoticed by Jason. 'Who's that?' he said.

'French teacher.' Jackie leaned in for a kiss. Jason sniffed, and just about managed a peck.

'Looks like a perv.'

'Oh, he's alright.'

'Been waiting ages.'

'Yeah, sorry. The bus didn't come.'

Jason looked Jackie up and down, and Jackie waited for his approval. He never actually said that she looked nice, or called her beautiful, just pointed out her faults. 'Trousers?' he said.

'Yeah, I thought with us going on the rides...'

He walked ahead of her, as if he didn't want to be seen

with her. Jackie caught up with him and linked arms. 'Hey,' she said, 'how about the chairoplanes?'

'Nah.'

'Well, I'd like to have a go.'

'Not in the mood really.' His nose wrinkled. 'You could have washed your hair. It stinks of cooking fat.'

'Sorry, I was so tired after standing up all day. By the time I'd had some tea, I didn't have time.'

'Didn't have time for your boyfriend?'

'It was really hard work, Jason. Dirty work.'

'Dirty.' He smirked. 'My dirty girlfriend.' He started sniggering.

A short distance away, The Count was watching the goings-on at a stall. A bloke was trying to throw a wooden hoop over a goldfish bowl, which stood on a bright green box. The hoop had to go right over the box to win a goldfish in a plastic bag of water. The hoops looked too small to fit over the stands. The Count's shoulders shook with laughter. He turned away from the stall and saw Jackie watching him. He raised the tip of his umbrella slightly, and nodded. Jason noticed this. 'He's following you,' he said. 'Told you he was a perv.'

Jackie was feeling the cold in her light jacket as the evening wore on. She started to shiver. They had done nothing but walk round the stalls and rides without going a single thing. 'Come on,' he said, 'Let's go onto the Downs.' Jackie knew what this meant; finding a dark place where they couldn't be seen. Jason was becoming more insistent as time went on. It had gone beyond unclipping her bra recently, beyond what she really wanted to do.

'Do you know what? No.'

'You what?'

'I'm saying no. You've been in a mood all night, called me dirty, and now you want to get amorous.'

Jason grabbed her arm. 'Don't be like that. Come on.'

She tried to pull her arm from his grip, but he was

stronger than her. She managed to break free, but he clamped an arm round her shoulder and pulled her in tight. He was walking fast, taking her with him, away from the fair and towards some trees. The lights from the rides and the fair faded; it was not so easy to watch her step, and Jackie's ankle turned in a rut in the mud made by tyre tracks. She stopped to rub her foot.

'You'll live,' Jason said.

'It hurts. I don't want to go any further.'

'Stop making such a fuss.' He grabbed her arm again and pulled her along.

'Jason, stop. I want to go home.'

'You don't know what you want. You'll like it, I promise.' He pulled her round to face him, kissed her hard and grabbed at her crotch.

'No, Jason. I said no.'

'Well I'm saying yes. I've waited long enough.'

Suddenly, a thwacking sound, and Jason let go of her. Jackie turned to see a familiar face, a man in a belted raincoat with a raised, rolled-up umbrella in his hand. Jason was nursing his shoulder.

'I think you have forgotten your manners, Monsieur,' The Count said to Jason. He lowered the spike of his umbrella onto Jason's chest and prodded him.

'Told you he was a perv,' Jason said to Jackie. 'Look at him in his flasher's raincoat. I saw you watching my girlfriend.'

The Count looked down his long nose at Jason. 'Jacqueline is my pupil,' he said. 'Elle a quinze ans.' Jason looked puzzled. 'Fifteen,' The Count said. 'Fifteen years old. And you are? No don't answer that. It is not I who is the pervert.'

'None of your fucking business what I do with my girlfriend.'

The Count snorted. 'It does not look to me like the young lady wants to go with you. C'est vrai, Jacqueline?'

Jackie nodded.

'OK. Time for you to go. Hop it,' he said to Jason.

'Huh, that's funny, from a fucking frog.'

The Count raised an eyebrow, and then his furled umbrella. 'Hop it, before I call the police.'

Jason retreated. He turned just once to shout, 'Fucking frog.' And then he disappeared into the crowd.

Jackie started sniffling. The Count handed her a large, monogrammed handkerchief from his pocket. It was embroidered with the letter H. 'Henri,' he said, 'Henri le Comte. The Count; I know that's what you call me.' At that moment, a few drops of rain began to fall. Jackie felt small and cold in her thin jacket. The Count opened his umbrella over the two of them. 'Mademoiselle, allow me to escort you. Would you like me to take you home?'

She thought of how she'd explain this, arriving home with her French teacher. 'No. No thank you. I can get the bus. I'd rather.' The sniffles had turned to sobs now. The Count stood politely by, holding the umbrella over both of them.

'I am guessing that you would like to compose yourself. When you are ready, I shall walk you to the bus stop and wait until you are safely on board.'

She zipped up her jacket as they passed the Grandstand. She would be back there tomorrow for another day's work.

She wondered what Kaz would say, what her mum would say, when she told them she had finished with Jason. Her mum would not be pleased, but Kaz would be. They would get paid on Saturday. Jackie could buy that top she'd seen with sleeves that Jason wouldn't have liked. She could go out dancing with her friends. She could be herself.

Another Woman's Kitchen

Brenda and Donald had been blessed with a corner house, and when Maggie Thatcher brought in the Right to Buy it from the council, they snapped it up. The big garden had been great when the boys were small, but now they could extend, make space for Simon, their youngest, and his wife. Teena, with a double 'e' rather than an 'i' – an affectation, when all was said and done, and a typical choice of name by her mother who walked round with her nose in the air. Brenda didn't hold with it, and wrote the wedding card to 'Simon and Tina,' spelt the proper way, claiming it was a slip of the pen when Simon pulled her up on it. She couldn't be doing with this Ms business either. What was wrong with being a Mrs? Ms sounds like Bzzz. And why get married when you won't take your husband's name?

The wedding had been a grand affair, two hundred guests, and though it's the bride's family that should stump up the money, Brenda and Donald had done their bit. Now they could help by providing a home for the kids. A wedding's all well and good, but a place to live – that's a gift for your child.

Simon and Teena lived in the house with Brenda and Donald while the building work went on, sleeping in Simon's room. The girl didn't lift a finger. Wet towels left on the floor … and the noise! Jesus, they didn't hold back, the two of them, even in the knowledge that his parents were sleeping on the same landing. Brenda stepped out of the bedroom once, when she heard their door open in the night, after a session of groaning and giggling and bedsprings bouncing. Teena in a scanty dressing gown, tripping along the corridor. 'Is someone sick?' Brenda had said. 'I wondered, what with the noise.' The girl just laughed, and flitted into the bathroom, her gown barely pulled closed, and she'd not a stitch on beneath.

Donald and Simon did the work on the extension, at weekends, after a long week on building sites, doing the same kind of work. To be fair and honest, there were bricks and sand and lengths of two-by-four that found their way from the site to home, just bits here and there that wouldn't be missed. It all helped. Meanwhile, Ms Teena, sat in the kiosk at Woolworth's, selling cigarettes, lighters and boxes of matches, picking at her nails and gassing to her friends in between serving the odd customer.

Brenda dropped the extension into the conversation whenever she could, especially when she was talking to Barbara next door, who hadn't even bought her council house, but lorded it up with the photo of her daughter in a graduation cap and gown on the mantelpiece. She'd say that the floors were being levelled, the windows chosen and about to be fitted, that there would be central heating. Barbara sniped behind her back, she was sure of it, but none of it hurt as, after all, Brenda had her child next door to her, whereas Barbara's grand grammar school and university daughter had moved to Scotland, and she hardly ever saw her grandchildren.

As the work went on, Donald and Simon put in a connecting door between the house and the extension. When the kids moved in, it gave Brenda a chance to roam at will while they were at work. Sure, Teena didn't mind at all if Brenda cleared the breakfast dishes and left them gleaming, draining next to the sink, or picked up the wet towels and dropped them in the machine, ran a cycle when she noticed that Teena hadn't bothered to do so, hung them out on the line, brought them in later and folded them, and never a word of thanks for any of it.

Brenda could still hear them at night, and on a Sunday afternoon – at it – for the walls weren't as thick as they might have been, and Simon bringing her a cup of tea afterwards, when she didn't do a thing for him. Spoilt, that Teena, and didn't know it. Living high on the hog, she was, holidays and meals out, and hardly ever cooked a dinner for Simon when he came home from a hard day's work. A freezer full of pizzas and ready meals in that new kitchen, built and paid for by Brenda and Donald. And half the time she sent Simon out for Chinese or chips. She wouldn't keep that figure for long at that rate.

Brenda hadn't had that much, when she and Donald started out, scarcely a stick of furniture to call their own, rented rooms, shared bathroom. Then, going back to her time in the children's home, she'd not much to call her own at all: clothes labelled, not even certain of getting your own knickers back from the laundry, smocks and shoes and socks provided, but nothing nice.

Few people knew about it, certainly not Barbara, nor about the child she'd had before she met Donald. Not even he knew about that. The one thing she'd learned was how to keep a good house, how to wash and scrub floors, how to iron shirts, and keep it all at bay, the thoughts that crept in if she allowed them to. So she didn't mind, really, that slip of a thing being slovenly, as it gave Brenda something to do after her few hours in the school kitchens and in the playground, watching the kiddies during breaks.

Still, she did hope for Granny duties. How handy it would be to have your grandchildren next door, how handy for Simon and Teena and for Brenda herself. A new lease of life, it'd give her. She watched the little ones at school, and thought how she'd love a little girl, like the child she'd given up, how she'd do her hair and buy her lovely clothes and toys. Colourful ribbons and hair slides, she'd buy. She'd only had brown ribbons at the children's home, and no-one had curled her hair or had it cut nicely. The clothes would be of soft stuff, not the rough material the smocks were made of. And there would be no-one forcing her grandchild onto her knees with a bucket and brush to scrub the floor. But then the thoughts were coming back, of those days, and the best thing to do would be to take down the nets and soak them in the sachets of whitener you could get at Woolworth's, to take her mind off it.

She'd seen Teena when she went in. Just a quick hello as she stopped to buy twenty Embassy at the kiosk. Teena was slouching behind the counter, hands propping up her chin, and Brenda said she'd really come in for the whitener, and would Teena like her nets done too? 'If you like, though I don't think they need it.' She signalled for the supervisor, a long lean streak of a lad. She wasn't allowed to serve family without someone checking, in case she undercharged, or didn't charge at all. He smarmed across, the cheek of him, said something about how she couldn't be Teena's mother-in-law, as she was too young. Brenda smiled in return, though she knew it was just flannel, and she looked every bit her age.

Simon was a late baby – she'd thought she was going through the change, assumed she was. They'd tried for children after the older boy, without success, and came to accept that Paul might be the only one. Brenda and Donald fell into enjoying one another – a good sex life, without the worry of babies or not, so Simon came as a surprise.

But she'd had a hundred of them, really, with the little ones at school that came and went, tiny infants that missed their mums the first week, clinging on to her skirt in the playground; then before you knew it, big enough to gang up and leave lone children crying at the edges of the playground, then on to big school.

She'd see them sometimes, in town, girls now pushing prams with toddlers in tow. 'Mrs B, you were our favourite dinner lady.' And Brenda would admire the kiddies, put a coin in the palm of the babies, for their money boxes. Hundreds of them.

Simon, he was the apple, he was. Paul long grown and gone, and no grandchildren from him, either. Simon was not the sharpest tool in the box, but good-hearted and eager, and just the sort of man that a girl like Teena could twist around her little finger.

Teena laughed rather too long at the long streak of a lad's jokes, then a sly smile, knowing, and she said to Brenda, 'See you later. Most probably.'

'You will,' said Brenda, 'And Simon. Your husband.' She glared at the lad as she snapped shut the clasp of her purse. She heard them giggling together as she left.

They used johnnies, so she found out. Condoms, they called them these days. All over the telly, it was, that advert with the iceberg. You could hardly work out what it was on about – AIDS. And then those programmes where they showed how to put them on bananas; not that she'd ever seen one with a bend in it! She wondered what they were doing with them, Simon and Teena, as she thought it was all about the Pill. They'd been married a while, and shouldn't they be thinking about kiddies by now? She kept her own counsel on this – she knew it wasn't right to push, and after all, until she found the johnnies, she wondered whether Teena might be having trouble conceiving, as Brenda had herself.

She'd found the johnnies in Teena's make-up bag. You'd think it would be down to the man, but then, on those programmes about the virus, the disease, they showed how you could make it more fun, sexier, if the woman put in on the man, with their mouths, even, and maybe that's what Simon and Teena went in for.

It had been curiosity that led Brenda to unzip the bag, to see what make-up the girl had. She couldn't even claim it had been left open with stuff spilling out, as it was in the back of a drawer underneath her knickers. Brenda knew she had no place looking in there, but it would be hours till anyone came home. She'd finished a pile of ironing, folded the clean towels and put them in the cupboard, and so she went for a prowl around.

Simon didn't seem happy, she thought, staying on for a drink after work, not in such a rush to come to his wife, and Brenda hated seeing him like that, she hated it. She knew she shouldn't interfere between a man and his wife, but she did speak to Donald about it, asked if he could shed any light, but he gave her a warning look and said, 'It's between the two of them.' There weren't rows as such, but there were times when he was out or she was out, and not so many when they were together and out.

Brenda was tired of waiting for the grandchild that she deserved and, who knew, if there were a pregnancy, it might bring the two close again. Accidents do happen, even with the Pill, even with those johnnies – nothing was a hundred per cent.

Brenda was in the extension on another afternoon, and looked in the back of the knicker drawer, unzipped the make-up bag, and there was only two where there had been three before, so they must have made it up. And then a thought – how those programmes had said they had to be snug – no air, no holes, or the sperm could get through. Infection could happen that way, and so could pregnancy. She took a needle from her sewing box, returned to the kids' bedroom, and made a tiny prick in each of the foil covers, through to the rubber beneath. She zipped up again, tucked the bag to the back of the drawer beneath the undies, and pushed the drawer shut.

Simon and Donald spent Good Friday and Easter Saturday doing some landscaping. There was a patio now, and the lawn had been turfed where the last bits of rubble had been from building the extension.

It was Brenda that suggested inviting Helen and Barry, Teena's parents, for Easter Monday. They'd bought a new garden set – table, chairs and a parasol, and Brenda decid-

153

ed on tea on the lawn, if the weather would hold. Scones and jam and cream with china cups and saucers from the best set. There'd be a time when they'd have to put them away, when a grandchild – maybe grandchildren – came along. It would be plastic cups and plates then.

The johnnies in Teena's bag had been restocked, so Brenda had done the deed again with her sewing needle. She expected news soon. Teena was looking a little heavier, she thought, and today would be the perfect opportunity to make an announcement. She'd been looking a bit subdued the last few days, and seemed unenthusiastic about afternoon tea. Brenda had consulted her about a cloth for the garden table, when she'd dropped by in Woolworth's, and she'd just shrugged. That supervisor had been hanging around the kiosk at the time, but there wasn't the laughter and joking that usually went on between them, and no false flattery towards Brenda either. In fact, Brenda could have sworn that Teena was close to tears. Hormonal, perhaps, and that would be natural if her suspicions were true.

Instructions had come through about decaf this and sweeteners that from Helen, and Brenda wondered should she try to bake some of the scones with sweetener, and would such a thing work? Teena's advice was sought again, but just another shrug.

Simon, too, was less communicative. He'd looked distracted for days, and when she'd asked if he was OK, and said he could talk to his mum about anything, the answer was, 'Don't push it, Mum,' while Donald gave a warning look over the top of his newspaper.

Still, she busied herself with the arrangements, and decided on a cloth rather than not, as they might have to hold the tea indoors if it rained. The day came, and the weather was fine enough to sit out. She rinsed the good plates but no doilies, as they were old-fashioned, and she had bought paper serviettes in a pale yellow to match the cloth, which had spring flowers around the edge. She didn't want to come across as having airs and graces, but she wanted everything to be just right.

Mid-morning, she heard raised voices through the wall. Not clear enough to work out what they were saying, and when it became apparent that Brenda had stilled herself next to the wall to listen in, Donald turned up the radio.

Helen and Barry parked on the road – a drive would be the next project for the men, meaning taking down a section of privet. Brenda explained this to them as they came in, ushering them straight to the patio and the table, laid with plates and cutlery. 'Someone's gone to a lot of trouble,' Helen said.

'No trouble at all,' Brenda said, straightening a cake fork next to one of her best plates.

'Where is she, your darling wife?' Helen asked Simon. Teena hadn't come out to greet her parents, but Simon stepped out of the French windows, accepting a back slap from his father-in-law and offering a peck on the cheek to Helen.

'Not feeling too well,' he said, staring down at the table with a frown. 'She's having a lie down. She'll be out later.'

Brenda's face fell. Her grand afternoon was falling apart. Or could it be the sickness? When she was expecting Simon, it was all day for the first few months. Even the sight of food would start her off. It was probably the smell of the baking.

'Shall I go in to her?' Helen said.

'She's dozing; maybe, in a bit.'

Brenda buzzed around with decaf coffee and scones and jam. It turned out the sweetener was for the coffee only; Helen tucked into the scones, made with ordinary sugar, and declared them delicious. She declined a third, patting her stomach, which looked as though scarcely a crumb of cake had passed through it in years.

Donald and Barry took off to discuss where the new

drive might best be placed, and how to tackle removing the hedge. Simon went to see if Teena was awake, leaving the two mothers to clear away the dishes. It was clouding over, and a wind was catching the edge of the cloth. Helen shook the crumbs from the cloth and folded it.

'I can't be sure,' Brenda said, 'but I'm wondering about Teena not feeling well. Whether there might be good news.' The cup that Helen was drying slipped from her grasp for a moment. She caught it before it hit the tiles. 'Surely not, not with how things are.' The colour had drained from her face. 'You must know they're having problems.'

'Problems?'

'Well, yes. The tests. Simon's low … you know.' Helen went back to drying the cups, vigorously balling a corner of the tea towel inside each one.

'Oh no, that can't be. He'd have said.'

'Very little chance of conceiving, apparently.'

Helen placed the last cup on the table and started on the cutlery. There'd be forks in with the knives, spoons in with the forks. The cake slice didn't belong in the cutlery drawer at all. There was space for it in the sideboard drawer. Everything would be topsy-turvy. It's what happened when a woman helped in another woman's kitchen. It would take a while to sort it all out.

Ivy Lodge

Two white cats sat either side of the gateposts, like sentries. Their eyes reflected in the headlights. And when I got out of the car and crouched down to stroke them, they fled.

Pete was in his garage, dressed in blue overalls spattered with oil. He raised a hand. 'Welcome, welcome.' He wiped his hands on a scrap of an old shirt, then threw it on the bench beside him.

'Your cats?'

'Yeah, little bastards.' If people match their pets, Pete was the exception. Large and dark, his stomach straining at his overalls, one strap tied in a knot to the bib where a button had come off. 'You got your keys?'

'Yes, thanks.' I started to unload my bags from the boot and the back seat of the car.

'Let me know if you need owt.' He turned his back and carried on pottering.

I couldn't stay in the house I'd shared with James, and Ivy Lodge was vacant and cheap. There wasn't a lot to unpack. I'm not one for trailing a childhood teddy bear, and it was a relief to walk away without the drag of marital furniture and dinner services; just a suitcase or two with my clothes, and my laptop. Ivy Lodge was furnished, so no worries about finding a bed or sofa, and the TV I could do without. Maybe I'd start reading all those books I'd never got around to. Join a reading group, perhaps.

I pushed against the heavy front door, a shoulder against it, my arms full of stuff. Pete peered across – halfway towards walking my way, but I shook my head, mouth set, lips pushed hard against each other, as if that would help the physical effort of opening the door. Remember to breathe, that's what they say in Pilates, breathe your way in to the pain, the posture, and as I breathed out, the door jerked slightly open. A heavy curtain hung behind it, too long for the door, gathered to one side and pooled across the floor like a bridal train. A pile of junk mail, too, was causing it to stick from underneath. Leaflets for Chinese and Indian takeaways and pizza houses, an A5 photocopied and stapled parish newsletter, which I put aside, and a couple of envelopes addressed to Sarah Flowers, who must have been a previous tenant. One looked like a bank statement, and I wondered why Sarah Flowers hadn't had her post redirected.

I tried to rearrange the door curtain to make my exit easier. It wouldn't draw completely to one side. I reached up to pull the rings over a connection in the rail. There was a slight rust to the copper-coloured rings. As I opened the door, one of the white cats slipped in, and ran into the bedroom. I decided to leave it for the moment, and left the door open as I brought Sarah Flowers' letters over to Pete.

His fingers were in a glass jar of metal washers, nails and screws. He raised his head, open-mouthed, as I approached, and showed him the letters. 'Oh, right. Just leave them there.' He nodded towards a space on the bench next to an oil can. A white cat snaked between his legs, its chin rubbing against his shin. He seemed unaware, as if it were an extension of him.

'The other one's come into the Lodge,' I said, gesturing towards the cat, now curling at his feet.

'Yeah, they do that. Any chance. Throw the blighter out.' He reached down and scratched the cat's ears, leaving a sooty mark on the white fur. The cat raised its head to meet his fingers.

'What are they called?'

'This one's Oscar, the other one's Fred. Fred's got a nick in one of his ears. Battle scar.'

Fred was curled on the bed when I returned to the Lodge. I shooed him away, but he just opened his eyes, then half-closed them, and settled down again. 'Come on, boy, you can't stay here.' I lowered my hand to scratch his ears, as I had seen Pete do with the other cat, but he reached out with his claws and scratched the back of my hand. I tried to open a window, so the cat could leave when he was ready, but the window wouldn't budge, so I called on Pete. Fred purred and rolled over to show his belly. Pete scooped him up, holding him like a baby. Fred narrowed his eyes at me as I showed both man and cat out of the door.

'Oh, I might as well put these leaflets in the recycling bin,' I said.

'Green bin out the back of the garage,' Pete said. As I lifted the lid, I saw the letters addressed to Sarah Flowers sitting on top of a pile of newspapers.

That first night in the Lodge, I had the strangest dream, though I didn't seem to be asleep. A weight was pinning me down, as if a creature were crouching on my chest. I wondered if one of the cats had somehow got back in, but there was no cat, nor anything else to cause that sensation. Logic told me it wasn't real, that it was a hangover from a dream that I couldn't quite recall on waking. But I had to admit that a sense of doubleness had been with me a while, an 'other' to the left of my vision. Perhaps my dead marriage was the cause, seeping in during the hours of darkness, catching me unawares when I thought I was do-ing so well on my own. I was cold, as I lay awake; it was so much colder in that room than the rest of the Lodge. I gathered my bedding and took it to the sofa. After that first night, I slept on the sofa every night, leaving the bed unused.

The hallway was dark; the front door had no window, and the only natural light came in when the doors to the other rooms were ajar. The bedroom was first, on the left, the bathroom a little further, on the right, and the living room straight ahead, with the kitchen branching off it. The windows were tall, sashed, and painted shut. The kitchen, with its cupboards and fittings crammed in, made me tense, like the feeling you get in a maze when you can't find your way out. At times, I felt squashed against the cupboards, the cooker, and the fridge, as if pushed slightly off-balance by unseen hands. There was a bricked-up doorway in the kitchen. Back in the days it was in use, it would have made the room all doors, with precious little space for anything else, but then there would have been another escape route, especially as the kitchen door handle often jammed, trapping me in the room.

I didn't mention the night visitation to Pete, or the feeling of confinement in the kitchen. But I did complain of the cold in the bedroom, of the doors sticking as if someone were pushing against them when I tried to open them.

As I put my key in the lock when I came home from work one evening, Pete opened the door. I complained that there was no rush for him to do the repairs, but he said he was just up the drive, and had nothing else to do that day. I got the impression that most days were like that for him. 'Well, young lady, I came around expecting to have to take the door off and plane it, but it opened as smooth as a swan on a lake.' He swung the door open and shut it several times to demonstrate. 'And the kitchen door handle … seems fine to me.' He beckoned me towards the kitchen; the handle that trapped me in there when I was alone dropped and rose with no resistance.

'Oh, I'm sorry to have bothered you,' I said, feeling foolish.

'No worries; that's what I'm here for. Funny thing is, the other girls who lived here, tenants I've had before you, complained about the door … and the handle in the kitchen.'

'Sarah Flowers? Did she complain?'

'Yeah, her.' He sniffed. 'Anyway, I've never had a problem with the doors. No meat on you, that's what it is. Need building up.' He smiled and winked. 'While I was here, I bled the radiators, but the one in the bedroom's proving stubborn.'

'It's always colder in there,' I said.

'If I can't manage to shift it, I'll get a plumber in.' He knelt on the floor, and gathered his tools into a canvas bag. He struggled to his feet. The folds of fat on his belly wobbled as he did so.

'Oh, the cupboard in the bedroom, it won't stay closed.' It was a ridiculous, shallow thing with a couple of hooks at the back.

'That one's a mystery,' he said. 'I've tried to take the door off and put some shelving in the alcove, but the screws in the hinges won't loosen.'

'I think it's damp,' I said. 'I hung some scarves in there and they got mottled with dark spots.'

'Same thing happened to the last tenant's stuff. But my dampness meter shows no damp.' He shrugged. 'You've got the wardrobe, though, haven't you? I'd just avoid using that cupboard. I like to think I'm Superman,' he raised his arms in a muscle man pose, 'but it seems I can't do everything.'

The cats were sitting on the outside sill of the bedroom window, pawing at the glass. 'Better go feed them, I suppose.' They jumped down, and were waiting outside the front door as Pete left. They tried to walk in, but he gently deflected them with a kick.

I joined a Pilates class. I had seen it advertised in the parish newsletter. Thought it would help tone me up, and maybe I'd meet some new people. Friends who knew James and me, as a couple, took sides when we split, or revelled in the drama of it all – terrible sympathy in their eyes, a touch on my arm. Unanswered calls, curt replies to emails saw some drift away. New start, new friends, but it turned out that the Pilates ladies were all friendly with one another. Five minutes before class was like the playground cliques at school; huddles formed around the hall, and whilst there were a few glances in my direction, it was as if there were 'no vacancies' signs posted by each group.

I returned to a cold house. I missed the welcoming light of the television; even the lights left on in all the rooms that drove me mad when I came home to James. He used to say that in every relationship there is one person who leaves all the lights burning while the other goes around switching them off. I now kept all the lights on, even in the rooms I wasn't using, as if the light could chase away the feelings of dread, discomfort. As if what happened in the dark, in that bedroom, could not be given dominion under the blaze of an electric light.

I went to the kitchen to get a snack: a couple of digestive biscuits with chocolate spread. I stopped by the mirror in the hallway first, looked at my profile, and sucked my belly in. The leggings and T-shirt I'd worn for exercising showed every lump and bump.

The biscuits looked bare, and not enough, so I tipped several more onto the plate, added peanut butter to those, sliced a banana and arranged the circles on top. I looked in the fridge, and there was a tub of double cream. I wouldn't have bought that – ever. I'd ordered online, and put the shopping away fast; maybe I didn't notice it, mistook it for my usual low-fat yogurt. It seemed a shame to waste it, and after all I had been exercising. I piled it onto the biscuits, and then spooned the rest of the tub of cream into my mouth.

The next day was tough; my manager was off sick, and I had to cover her phone, her work, as well as my own. But when I came home, the door didn't stick at all. At least something had gone right that day.

I dumped my bag and coat on the bed. It was still so cold in the bedroom, even though it was June. I guessed these old buildings take a while to warm up, even in the summer. North facing, probably.

I noticed a letter, caught in the folds at the foot of the curtain that hung at the door. The postmark was from the week before. The seal on the envelope was bumpy, as if the glue had come away, and it was only stuck at the point of the flap. I recognised my Aunt Tina's handwriting. She was one of the few people who still wrote by hand, never quite trusted the new; emailing wasn't her thing.

I sat with a coffee, and tucked my feet up beside me on the sofa, ready for a newsy read. Pages later, I learned that she was coming to stay at the weekend. I phoned her, said I'd only just got the letter, and asked if she was still coming, as she hadn't heard from me. 'I've no spare room,' I said, hoping to put her off.

'You have a sofa, don't you?'

'A sofa bed, yes.' My bed. I'd not slept in the bedroom since that first night.

'I'll see you on Friday evening. The sofa bed will be good enough for me.'

I decided to sleep in the bedroom that night; it was time to toughen up. But when it came to it, I chickened out, and slept on the sofa as usual. I'd offer Tina the bedroom; insist on it.

I ordered some extra shopping online, and it arrived early on the Friday, just before I left for work, so I put the carrier of chilled stuff in the fridge, and dashed out the door.

Tina arrived before I got back from work, and Pete spotted her sitting in her car. He asked her if she'd like a cup of tea at the big house, which she declined, but accepted his offer of letting her into the Lodge with his key. She told me later that Pete was a little too familiar for her liking. He had followed her in, showed her around, then sat chatting on the sofa until I came home. Both cats had trailed after him, and had leapt onto the kitchen surfaces, sniffing in the Sainsbury's bags of shopping I had left that morning.

'He seems rather comfortable in your house,' Tina said. 'Too comfortable.'

I shrugged. 'He's been in a fair amount to do some maintenance. He's all right, really.'

'Hmmm. Does he not disturb you? When you have, you know, company?' She winked.

'Oh, there's nothing like that. No-one.'

'You're a young woman. Don't deprive yourself. Not that there can be many opportunities to meet men out in the sticks. Or maybe Pete thinks he's in with a chance?' I laughed. 'He might not be your cup of tea,' she said, 'But you may well be his. I would watch out, if I were you.'

When I unpacked the food delivery, there was stuff I hadn't ordered. The deliveryman must have given me a bag of someone else's shopping by mistake. But there were things in there that Tina and I enjoyed that evening: chocolate, strawberry cream tarts, crème caramels and wine. Well, the wine I had ordered, for sure. And we sat up late, talking, snacking and drinking. There was some haggling over the bed, but Tina agreed to take it, in the end, and left me to the sofa.

During the night, I saw a parallelogram of light cast from the bedroom onto the hall carpet. I heard Tina use the bathroom; saw her stand a while in the hall, then the light diminished to a thin beam as she partially closed the bedroom door. The light stayed on all night, and when I asked her how she had slept, she said she'd had a bad dream, so she'd sat up reading. She looked pale, her eyes circled with dark, and I nearly said something, nearly asked about the dream.

'Look, why don't I treat us to a night in a hotel?' she said. 'It would do you good to get you out of here for a while.' She meant *get you out of this dingy place*. I could tell what she thought by the way her nose wrinkled, her frown. The air was stale. I'd become used to it, the mustiness. I hate those scented fresheners, and I did get some air in through the slim window in the bathroom, which was jammed open, though the ivy from the wall outside was inclined to creep in.

I shook my head. 'To be honest, Auntie, I've got a lot of work to catch up on; my manager's been off sick, and I'm covering for her.'

'Never mind your manager; you're not looking so well yourself.'

'I'm fine,' I said. Knowing that the reflection in the hall mirror told me otherwise.

'To be honest, love, I don't know what you're doing here. There's something … uncomfortable about this house. It's sucked you in, the idea of deprivation, of living like a student with a creepy landlord.'

I wasn't offended by what she said, just kind of blank about it. She gave me a hug, and suggested I look for somewhere to stay on my 'online thingy'. She'd seen a bed and breakfast sign not far outside the village, and we quickly found the number and booked.

It was rather lovely to sleep in a proper bed that night, with clean sheets and fluffy towels in the en suite, and in a room with a window that opened to let the air in. Tina and I shared a room, and even with her snoring gently in the next bed, I slept better than I had in months.

I opted for the full English at breakfast and several cups of tea. 'Now you look better,' Tina said, and I managed a smile.

I'd seen the landlady in the village shop, and she too recognised me. 'You're fairly new, aren't you?' she said. I nodded, said I'd moved into Ivy Lodge. She stopped clearing the plates from the table for a second. 'Oh … how are you finding it?'

'It suits me for now,' I said. Tina grimaced, and exchanged a glance with the landlady.

'It's just … and perhaps I shouldn't mention it … that

quite a few young women have rented the place. They don't stay long.'

'Sarah Flowers…'

'Yes, she was there before you. We used to have a chat in the shop. Nice girl. Left all of a sudden. And others before her.' She stood for a moment by the table, as if there was more to tell, then quickly gathered the rest of the crockery.

'I really think you should move on,' Tina said.

'I will, in time. But I've signed a contract. I can't leave yet. Besides, I don't know where I want to be.'

When I returned to the Lodge later that day, there was more post for Sarah Flowers. I added the envelopes to the pile of letters I had collected, intending to mark them 'return to sender'. Then I went to the fridge. We hadn't eaten half of the food I'd got in for Tina's visit, not to mention the extra stuff that was delivered by mistake. I threw the cream cakes in the bin. I knew I wouldn't eat just one, it would be all four, so it would be better to get rid of the lot. Later, I picked the box out of the bin and ate them all.

I tried to sleep in the bedroom that night. The temperature had risen in the other rooms, as the summer progressed. But there was still a chill in that room, so I kept the winter duvet on. During the night, it felt as though a hand suddenly snatched the cover from the bed. I could still feel the weight of it on me, and more, as if a there were a pile of duvets on top of one another, on top of me, but I was shivering. And when I went to pull the duvet tighter around me, it wasn't there at all. It was heaped on the floor.

I decided to move the furniture around. Perhaps by tackling the bedroom I would get rid of that feeling of dread, the reluctance to use it. There wasn't a lot to work with in the Lodge, not much space, and the furniture was heavy. So I called on Pete to help.

Oscar followed Pete in, and while we moved from one room to another, discussing where to put the furniture, I saw the cat squat on the bed and piss on it. 'Pete, quick,' I shouted. Oscar yowled as Pete chased him into the hallway and shooed him out of the front door. 'Little bugger,' Pete said.

I filled the washing up bowl with water and disinfectant and scrubbed at the mattress. 'Least I can do is get you a new mattress,' Pete said. 'And while we're at it, we'll give the room a lick of paint.' I sighed, close to tears. 'All a bit much, is it, love?' He offered me a greying handkerchief. 'Could you manage on the sofa a night or two?' he said. I nodded, sniffing back my tears. 'Right, let's go and choose some paint, and make a start today.'

Pete and I tipped the mattress this way and that as we struggled to get it out into the narrow hallway and through the front door. Pete said he'd move around the chest of drawers and wardrobe as he painted. There was a mark on top of the chest – a scratch like claw marks, quite deep, and a stain on the wall behind it, dark and indistinct. The shallow cupboard would stay as it was; maybe he'd hammer it shut, Pete said, or put the wardrobe in front of it.

When we shifted the mattress out of the house, the postman handed me a letter. 'Who's that from?' Pete asked.

'Shan't know until I open it,' I said, placing it on the coffee table. When I came to read it later, it was in the kitchen, next to the kettle. It was from Tina. She was offering me money, enough for a deposit on a house. 'No point keeping it in the bank when you could do with it,' she wrote. 'Besides, I'll look on it as an investment; I'm counting on you to look after me in my old age!' I mentally filed it as something to think about after the decorating was complete. I had little time on my own, to think, as Pete was around for several days.

He finished the skirting boards on a Saturday afternoon. There was just the doorframe to do, and he said he'd work on into the evening. 'I'm going to the chip shop,' he said, and he came back with a large piece of haddock and a mega size portion of chips that we split, eating from the polystyrene carton with wooden forks and swigging from cans of Coke that he'd carried in the pockets of his fleece. I found a tub of ice cream in the freezer, which we polished off between us, and sat in companionable fullness for a while before he got on with the work. I was in joggers and an old T-shirt, not wanting to get paint on my good clothes, but my good clothes were getting tighter in any case. It mattered less, how I looked, as the months passed. I'd been working from home – a new policy of hot-desking meant I'd lost my base in the office. Days could go by without stepping outside. I forgot to brush my hair unless I caught my reflection before I had to go to a meeting.

I'd emptied the wardrobe to make it easier to move, and piled the clothes onto the floor. The white shirt and black trousers I'd worn with James on our last anniversary, when we had sat on opposite sides of a restaurant table, and had nothing to talk about; the mistake of the dress bought for a wedding with the large blue roses printed on it. And there were so many skirts that had once sat loose on my waist, which I could only do up with the aid of a large safety pin across the gaping top of a zip. A charity collection bag came through the door, and I filled it, plus two black sacks besides. Perhaps I would become like whoever had lived in the lodge in the olden days. Two dresses, worn in rotation, hung on the hooks at the back of the cupboard.

'This wardrobe, it takes up so much space,' I said to Pete as he worked around it to paint the wall.

He turned as best he could to look at me, with the wardrobe in his way. I noticed the stain on the wall, which still showed through where Pete had painted; it would need another coat. 'Hmm, it's been here as long as I remember, that wardrobe.' He kicked the back of it with his heel.

'Maybe I'd get a bit for it. Some people like this old stuff. Get you something modern, lighter.'

I placed an ad on Gumtree, and a couple came to collect the wardrobe. I wondered how it had ever got into the room; furniture didn't come flat-packed in the days when that was made. Try as they might, it wouldn't go through the bedroom door and turn the corner down the hallway. Pete had to refund the money, and the wardrobe stayed. The stain on the wall had been resistant to three coats of Raspberry Diva paint, so the wardrobe was placed in front of it. Lifting the carpet had also revealed that the stain spread to the floorboards below the wall. It spread as far as where the bed stood.

The room smelt of fresh paint for a while, but the mustiness didn't lift. On the night when I made up the new bed and slept in the room, there was a feeling of closeness, like the days before a thunderstorm when heat builds and you long for rain. It felt like anger.

Marks appeared on all the clothes I hung in the wardrobe, as if the stain on the wall was transferring to them. I scrubbed them, put stain remover in the washing machine, but they wouldn't come out. There was nowhere outside to hang washing, so they were draped over an airer for days, and never felt fully dry.

'You can use my washing line if you like,' Pete said, one day, as I was setting off for a meeting. 'I went in to see if I'd left my hammer behind, and saw you had wet clothes hanging indoors.' The dress I was wearing was pockmarked and smelled of mildew. I was ill-prepared for the meeting. Sleep had left me; I rested on the sofa in a half-doze at nights, getting up to the fridge for snacks that I hardly remembered eating. The floor would be strewn with wrappers in the morning, and I would scoop them into the bin. Waking and sleeping became one. Pete had entered my dreams, with the white cats trailing behind him as he wandered through the Lodge.

More letters arrived for Sarah Flowers. A small pile of them accrued, and occasionally they would disappear, after Pete had let himself in under some pretext or other. Tina's letter also went missing; it had been at the bottom of a number of bills and letters offering me loans and credit card balance transfers.

A month went by before Tina turned up at my door. By that time, I'd become obsessed with the wardrobe. How had it ever got into that room? It creaked, and once there was a scratching from within. When I opened it, a cat flew out. Fred – I noticed the nick in his ear that distinguished him from Oscar.

'It's the wardrobe,' I said to Tina, before she had the chance to say hello. 'Maybe someone added a hollow panel at the back; there will something in there, I swear.'

Tina took off her jacket and draped it over a chair. 'What are you on about?'

'The wardrobe.'

'Yes, what about it?'

'It got bigger. That's why we couldn't get it out of the room.'

She frowned, and looked me up and down. 'Will it set your mind at rest if we check?' I nodded. 'Tape measure?' There was a metal rule, the kind that retracts into a case, which Pete had left in the Lodge. Tina measured inside the wardrobe, from the door to the back board, then along the outside. The difference was negligible. 'It was built in this room,' she said. 'They probably didn't think about getting it out. Furniture was made to last back then.'

My shoulders drooped. I'd imagined a hidden space, something within that would explain the goings on in that room.

'But I didn't come to talk about wardrobes,' she said, heading for the kitchen to put the kettle on. 'My letter; you haven't replied.'

'No, sorry.' I had put it to the back of my mind. When

Pete wasn't around, I'd mainly thought about the wardrobe, or if the cats were a malign influence.

'I've brought some house details. That's if you want to stay in the village. Might be better to move on.'

It seemed impossible to leave; Ivy Lodge contained me. Pete brought me takeaways, so I hardly shopped for food anymore. The kitchen bin was overflowing with foil containers and lidded plastic pots. I forgot to take the rubbish out in time for bin days; I forgot which days the bins were emptied. Work was getting impatient. There was talk of disciplinary proceedings. My boss suggested I see a doctor, but that would mean leaving the house.

'It's not what you imagined, this life of freedom, is it?' I shook my head. 'But it will be … you just need to get away from here.'

We returned to the B&B that night, after Tina had helped me clean the kitchen and take the rubbish out. She closed the doors firmly on the wardrobe and the bedroom before we left. She spoke to Pete before we set off. I remained in the car, but could hear them talking. 'How could you let her get like this?'

'Like what?'

'She's huge, for a start, and she hasn't seen daylight for weeks.'

He picked up and put down a succession of tools on the workbench, avoiding her gaze. 'Looks better with some weight on her, if you ask me. I bring her food, keep an eye.'

'You know the story, of course,' the landlady of the B&B said as she served us breakfast next morning. 'Servant girl, all but held captive, back in the day.'

'No, I had no idea,' I said.

'Oh yes, it was quite a horror story. She worked for the man at the big house; only went between Ivy Lodge and the house, never any further. And the man … forget his name … well, they'd call it coercive control these days. Fed her, clothed her, locked her in the Lodge, had his wicked way with her. She'd come to depend on him, see? Found dead in the end.'

Tina went pale. 'How did she die?'

'Bled to death. A baby's corpse was found in the wardrobe, wrapped. Stillborn, they reckon. I doubt she had any help with the birth.'

'Gruesome,' said Tina. 'Poor thing.'

'A couple of cats found her, they say. Some exotic breed owned by the man at the big house. They kept scratching at one of the windows – it wouldn't close properly, as the ivy crept in from the outside wall. The clattering of the window catch brought the gardener to it, and he saw the poor girl through the bedroom window.'

'You felt it, too, didn't you?' I said to Tina, after the landlady had cleared the table. 'When you stayed over. In that room.'

Tina stared at the table cloth. 'Let's go and see some of these houses,' she said. She'd brought the brochures to the breakfast table. 'And then we'll go and pack your things.'

As I rose from my chair, the fluttering that I'd felt in my belly for some weeks became a definite kick.

Caged

The Neanderthal's dog had been barking all day. When the neighbours' car pulled up outside that evening, Ellen went out to have a quiet word, a considered word, but when it came to it, the words came out loud and furious. Why keep a dog? Why cage it in the garden? Why do this, day after day, torturing the animal and the neighbourhood?

'Do you want us to have it put down, then?' Cherie, the Neanderthal's wife, said as she ushered their daughter towards the house.

'No, of course not,' said Ellen, 'but maybe there's someone who'd like a dog. Someone who would care.'

The Neanderthal stepped close, towering over her, then turned away, moving to unload a case of lager from the boot. 'If you don't like it, move.'

Move? Wasn't she the homeowner and they the ones renting? She'd call their landlord, that's what she'd do, just as soon as she'd calmed down. Meanwhile, the barking had stopped. Poor dog. Poor Max. He was so sweet when he was let out of his cage and into the garden. Cherie or Lisa, the daughter, would do that, when the Neanderthal was out. Max would lick Ellen's hand with his slobbering tongue through the trellised fence when she offered her palm to him. She'd considered kidnapping Max, drawing him over the fence, all several slathering stones of him, and taking him to a shelter, but she'd heard that some euthanized the dogs they couldn't place. And surely the Neanderthal would suspect her role in Max's disappearance.

Cherie, she was OK; she'd look after Max better if it weren't for the Neanderthal's bullying, and as for Lisa, the lack of a teenager's noise through the thin walls was not natural. In fact the only sounds were the Neanderthal kick-starting his lungs in the morning and punctuating every sentence with the word 'Fucking'. Ellen could take him off perfectly, imitating his phlegmy cough and 'Fucking ... fucking ... fucking'. It was only funny as long as he didn't overhear her, so she kept her performances to the kitchen, where the walls were thicker. The two houses were mirror images of each other; kitchen backed on to kitchen, bedroom to bedroom, stairs spreading downwards in opposite directions from the upstairs landings.

The walls were only one brick thick, except for in the kitchen. Ellen had discovered this when her builder accidentally knocked a hole in her bedroom wall, and daylight from the Neanderthal's house shone through. Not wanting to face him, Ellen persuaded the builder to go round to apologise, with a promise to make good. She could hear the full exchange through the walls. 'I've had enough of it,' the Neanderthal shouted, 'All this fucking noise. You can fuck off out of it.'

Minutes later, Cherie called over the garden fence. 'These things happen ... as long as you put it straight.' She smiled at the builder, arranged a time for him to do the work. 'My husband, he don't mean it; he's a pussycat, really.' Anyone less like a pussycat Ellen could not imagine. Though the silence that reigned much of the time he was home brought to mind a lion, padding round his lair, roaring when he wanted to show his power.

She wished the Neanderthal dead, and there were moments when it seemed it might happen, that he would clutch at his chest and fall. He looked so purple and bloated that he could be rolled and burst for juice, and he seemed to have trouble walking. Then she learned that bits of him were dropping off. Toes.

He'd had a wound that wouldn't heal. Diabetes, Cherie told her. You had to look after your feet with that. You had to look to your diet as well, and Ellen couldn't imagine him sticking to beansprouts and tap water.

'They call it the silent killer,' Cherie said. She was hanging out the washing, three days after leaving hospital herself. The loss of the Neanderthal's toes coincided with her having a hysterectomy. Ellen protested that she shouldn't be doing the housework, should be putting her feet up. 'I'm all right,' Cherie said. 'Lisa carried the basket out for me.' Ellen had seen that smile before, fixed to tell herself that everything was fine.

She was wearing a spaghetti-strapped top and leggings. Her face was made up, just to walk down the garden. Such a pretty woman, her body round but attractive in all the right places; such a waste, tied to a man like that. The Neanderthal hobbled out of the back door, his foot bandaged, steadying himself with a walking stick. 'Better get in,' she said. 'He'll be ready for a cup of tea.'

The next morning, Ellen opened her bedroom curtains and saw Cherie below, in her garden, wearing a fluffy dressing gown with pink hearts on it, smoking a cigarette. Her smile was absent, with no one to fix it for. A moment to herself, away from the house – just yards away – away from his coughing and smoking and swearing, but still within the confines of her garden, near the cage where the dog spent most of his days and nights.

All was quiet on New Year's Eve as Ellen went to bed. Forced to go to neighbourhood parties in other years, she had watched as the married and attached reached for each other at midnight. It was more than she could bear, to watch from the sidelines, or worse, be grabbed by some drunken individual.

Once, when the fashion was for fireworks as the year turned, the various neighbourhood parties decanted into the street to watch the display, and Nick from number 56 grabbed her as the chimes of midnight rang. He'd been leering at her for months, ever since her divorce, and that night, that New Year's Eve, he'd followed her into the party and grabbed her for a slow dance, held her indecently close. She'd reacted with all the passion of an iron-ing board, and he'd never bothered her since.

But that was in her old neighbourhood, when she was still in what the solicitors quaintly referred to as the mari-tal home. In this new place, this village, people left her alone.

This New Year's Eve, she slept through the turning of the year. It was dark when she woke, except for the green digits on the clock glowing 03.15. A thud, as if a body had hit the wall in the bedroom next door, a female whisper, as if pleading, a cold whimper, then silence.

She lay with her eyes wide open, fingers clutching the duvet. She wondered whether to let things be, now it was quiet, but she would not be able to live with herself if something terrible had happened. She crept down to the kitchen to make the call, so as not to be overheard. Was it an emergency? Yes. 999. She was shaking as she dialled the number. It would be a while, the operator said. The police were very busy. No doubt there were hundreds of such calls, violence at home, fighting in the streets.

Ellen made a camomile tea and sat on the sofa. She waited for the police to arrive. She'd see the lights of their vehicle through the curtains; hear them knock at the house next door. But there were no headlights, no knock, nor any voices to be heard on the other side of the wall. She lay on the sofa with a blanket pulled over her and fell into a deep sleep. Had the police come by and found no reason to knock at a dark and quiet house? Perhaps they had not come at all. Then she saw Cherie out with the dog late morning. She wasn't close enough to notice any bruising, a black eye, perhaps. She was, at least, alive. The noise, then the silence – that had been hard to take. The silence was in some ways more terrible.

When Ellen came back from a few days away, the dog's cage in the neighbours' garden stood in pieces, leaning against the brick wall. The curtains were drawn next door, remained closed for days then weeks.

For a while, she tensed when a car slowed outside, or when she heard the letterbox slamming in the house next door, only to see the postman walking up the path. And then she came to believe that the neighbours weren't coming back, that she had gained the peaceful life she had longed for when she moved to the village.

She started to turn up the volume of the television. Sometimes, she sang to herself, or talked back to the presenters on the radio. It gave a semblance of company, of there being someone else in the house.

When she phoned her sons, they were often about to go out, or were in meetings, or lost reception on their mobiles as they went into tunnels, busy going places, as she had encouraged them to do as they grew up. They said they would call her back, but seldom did. Ellen told herself that she liked the solitary life, the freedom from the demands of other people, but sometimes it was just too quiet.

Just as she became used to the silence, stopped expecting the sounds of swearing, or coughing or stomping about, there came one afternoon a clattering, a door being slammed in the house next door. Ellen's doorbell rang, and Cherie stood on the doorstep, smiling. Ellen invited her in. She sat in the armchair, cradling a cup of coffee. 'Thought I'd tell you what's been happening,' she said. Ellen waited as she slugged deep from her drink. 'About Neil.' Ellen wondered who Neil was – of course, the Neanderthal; his name was Neil. 'His toes, they wouldn't heal. And his leg became ... well, it started to smell.'

'God, how awful,' Ellen said.

'He wouldn't be seen by a doctor, wouldn't go to the hospital, but Lisa begged him. Said she was afraid of what might happen. But you know what he's like.' Ellen nodded. 'So I called an ambulance. He complained and swore, said he didn't need no hospital. Didn't do too much for his temper, but he was in so much pain. Then there was a right kerfuffle when they turned up. He didn't want to let them in the house. They told him straight, what would happen if he didn't get treatment … you know … so he agreed to go. They amputated, from the knee, the next morning.'

Ellen offered a biscuit. She couldn't think what else to do. She imagined the Neanderthal swearing at the nurses, the other patients, all of them dreading his next outburst.

'He's happy as Larry now; he's not in so much pain, see? But we couldn't come back here, not with the stairs.' They had been staying with his mother, dog and all, waiting for the Council to find them a suitable place. Cherie had come back to pick up the post, to pack up the last of their things.

'I'll give you our new address,' she said. Ellen opened a drawer to get a notepad and pen. The leaflets were in there, the ones she'd picked up in case Cherie should need them. There was help for women like her, for children like Lisa. Shelters, relocation, away from men like him. She put her hand on the leaflets for a second. 'I hope you'll be all right,' Ellen said, as she handed the pad and pen to Cherie.

'We'll all be fine,' Cherie said. How small she looked, how broad her smile. Later, Ellen transferred the new address and phone number into her address book, knowing that she would never use them.

Weary of the voices on the radio, she unlocked the door and stepped into the yard. There was a spit of rain in the air. She didn't bother with the old coat she kept on a hook by the back door, just slipped into the shoes that stood beneath it. She walked to the fence, to the particular square in the trellis through which the dog used to poke his head. So hungry for attention that he lapped it up, he couldn't get enough, and she too was happy in those moments. The shiver in his back in anticipation of her touch, the velvet of his ears, the thick trails of saliva he left on her hands, then the howling as she left him. But now, the only sound was the wind and a hard rain hitting the windowpanes of the shed.

For a Rainy Day

Margaret kept coins in coffee jars. A bit here and there, squirreled away for a rainy day. She saved change for Sonia's dinner money, so she would have the right amount on a Monday morning. And for when Jim-the-milkman collected on a Friday. Window cleaner, once a month, and for paying the man from the Pru.

Eventually, Sonia left school, United Dairies stopped their rounds due to supermarket milk, and bills got paid through the bank. But Margaret kept up her habit of collecting change in jars for a rainy day. And for an escape route, should she need it. If things got bad with Ted. Again.

She stored the jars behind a loose panel at the back of the kitchen units, in case of burglary. And in case of Ted. The one place he would never look, not being one for noticing loose panels, or for going into the kitchen, except for making tea. And a mess.

Margaret began adding notes to the coins – a fiver here, a tenner there – saved from the housekeeping and from selling at boot fairs; bits and bobs that Ted never noticed when they were there, or when they were gone. After a while, Margaret stopped emptying the jars, just screwed the lids on when they were full and pushed them a little further along the space behind the loose panel, stacked them several jars high till they scraped the bottom of the worktop that concealed them.

In the weeks following Ted's funeral, Margaret reached far into the space behind the loose panel, took out all the jars and counted the contents. A tidy sum. She dealt with coins and notes that were going out of circulation by giving them to her grandchildren. She had always given them something for their piggybanks when they visited, and cash for birthdays and Christmas, and this was just a bigger gift. Then Sonia said that vouchers were better for birthdays and Christmas, so the jars were just added to as time went on, nothing taken out.

It had always been Margaret's secret, the jars behind the loose panel. She only went to them when alone in the house, when she was sure of not being disturbed. And while she had made a will, before her memory started to play tricks on her and she began to mistake Sonia for her mother at times, she never told a soul about the jars.

The house fetched a good price, after Margaret died. Astonishing, really, considering what she and Ted had paid for it in 1969. It needed updating, of course – new kitchen and all. That loose panel had never been fixed, yet the jars remained undiscovered. A nice little nest egg for someone, you'd think. The builders, perhaps, or the new owners. But no, they found it charming, the vintage style. They would even keep the chocolate brown bathroom suite; wouldn't change a thing.

Margaret's jars were safe. She liked to visit sometimes, when no-one was around, when she wouldn't be discovered. To take the jars out and count the notes and coins, screw on the lids and put them back. She never knew when she might need the money. For a rainy day.

How Beautiful

Ed touched two fingers on the entry screen, but the door remained shut. He wiped his fingers on his jeans, and tried again. Red neon letters flashed ACCESS DENIED. He sighed; technology, as advanced as it was, still needed turning off and back on again sometimes. He swiped the house icon on his tablet, but the screen flashed the same as the entry panel by the door: ACCESS DENIED.

He signalled to the uniformed man beyond the glass door by raising his tablet and pointing to the words on the screen. The man was reclining in a chair behind a desk, tipped as far as you could an ergonomic tip-proof chair, in the manner of an under-worked sheriff in an old Western movie, his peaked cap over his eyes. The heels of his scuffed cowboy boots were up on the desk. He dropped his feet to the floor, and the chair brought him upright. He drew the cap back on his head, and spoke into a microphone. 'The screen is on your left.'

Ed tried as hard as he could to signal back: waved a finger, shook his head. The grille where the man's voice came out was too high and Ed's voice too weak to reach it. The man shrugged his shoulders and walked to the door. He opened it to the electronic equivalent of a door being stopped by a security chain. 'What's the problem, Sir?' He surveyed Ed, frown lines on his forehead. Ed swiped the house icon on his tablet. ACCESS DENIED flashed red. The man harrumphed, opened the door, stepped outside and closed it again, then tried his own fingers on the entry panel by the door. PROCEED flashed in green, accompanied by the familiar three-toned chime. He stopped the door opening all the way with a series of two, three and one-fingered taps on the panel. The door reset to security-chain.

'Your access has been denied,' he said.

Ed tried to find a polite way of saying, 'No shit, Sherlock'. He had the suspicion that men in uniforms didn't get sarcasm, most of all those who wore cowboy boots and tipped their chairs like Wild West sheriffs. Instead he said, 'Could you tell me why?'

'Sorry, lad, couldn't get that; say again.'

Ed sighed and wrote the words on his tablet, then offered it to Mr Wild West. The man pressed the house icon. 'It says access denied.'

'I know that; can you tell me why?'

'Sorry, couldn't understand that either. Tell you what, I'll try and find out why, if you like.' Ed pursed his lips and breathed out through his nostrils. He nodded. The man performed a three- two- one-fingered passcode on Ed's tablet, pressed one thing and another, his brow furrowed. 'Your access is denied,' he said, somewhat unnecessarily, adding, 'You've been reassessed and you're no longer eligible.'

'I know I've been reassessed, but what's that got to do with where I live?' Wild West looked bewildered. Ed was used to this – people who had trouble listening. He could speak a little louder, but he doubted that it would make any difference. Some people just couldn't tune in. He remembered the card in his top pocket, and offered it to Wild West. 'They gave me this at the validation centre, but my tablet won't read it.'

'No, didn't get any of that. I could try reading your card, see if that tells us any more.' He scanned the card with his wrist-reader. 'Bernard 451 Yellow.'

'Bernard?'

'Yep, Bernard 451 Yellow.' At last, Wild West had understood one word of Ed's speech. 'Bernard is one of the new categories.'

'OK, so what do I get for being a Bernard?'

'I'll see what you get for being a Bernard, shall I?' He looked at his wrist-reader, puffing out his cheeks as he did so: 'Vouchers.'

'I used to get money paid into my bank.'

Wild West shook his head, then looked as if he'd had a eureka moment. 'Money – I heard you say money. Getting better at this, aren't I?' Ed attempted an encouraging smile. Wild West went back to peering at the reader. 'Yellows aren't allowed currency. Try checking your bank balance.' Ed tapped the £ icon on his tablet. ACCESS DENIED flashed in red letters, alternating with BERNARD 451 in yellow. 'See, vouchers is what you'll get,' Wild West said. 'Have you tried your email? They might have sent a message.' Ed pressed the envelope icon: ACCESS DENIED.

'I'll try the back-up account..' Ed touched the icon that showed a sheet of paper and a quill pen with an inkpot by the side. ACCESS DENIED. 'This is ridiculous. I need to get into my apartment. I couldn't get in round the front, that's why I tried this door.'

'Have you tried the front door?' Wild West said. Ed decided to save his breath, and just nodded. 'No luck?' Wild West said. Ed shook his head. 'ACCESS DENIED' they said together. Wild West sniffed. 'You've got a problem, my friend. Let's take a look at your tablet. He scanned it with his wrist-reader, returned the tablet to Ed and lifted his wrist toward his mouth, cupping his hand over his ear.

'Lola? Quentin here.' Ed stifled a giggle. Quentin was not a name that went with cowboy boots. Quentin looked at him sharply. 'Not bad, Lola, not too shabby. You?' Ed drummed his fingers on his tablet. Every icon turned yellow, one by one – the £, the envelope, the paper, quill and inkpot - then ghosted to a pale lemon. He held it up for Quentin to look at. Quentin's eyes narrowed. 'I've got a chap here who's getting ACCESS DENIED.' He took Ed's tablet. 'Yep: Bernard 451 Yellow. Yellow, yes.' He looked at Ed, then turned his back on him, opened the door and went inside carrying the tablet. The door closed behind him.

'Hey, my tablet,' Ed said. Quentin took a wand from

beneath the desk and waved it over the screen. The blue light that flashed at the top of the device when it was active dulled, and then died. Ed shifted in his seat, pushed the reverse button on the arm of his chair, but nothing moved. He tried to shift the wheels with his hands, and looked down to see them clamped like an illegally parked car, with mini yellow clips that were rooted into slots in the pavement. 'Hey, Quentin!' He shouted as best he could and waved. He tried to raise the seat to standing – sometimes it helped to talk eye to eye – but that didn't work either. Quentin continued to talk to his wrist, glancing in Ed's direction, but not so Ed could catch his eye. His throat felt constricted and his breath came in gasps.

A large vehicle drew up, yellow with blacked-out windows, and a woman stepped out of the driver's door. She was wearing a helmet with a visor covering her face. Quentin came out to greet her, ensuring that the door closed behind him. 'What's going on?' Ed said. Quentin remained tight-lipped. 'Can I have my tablet back, please?'

Quentin nodded at the woman. 'Lola.'

She lifted her visor. 'Quentin,' she said, as she moved to the front of Ed's chair, her booted feet up against the wheels, one either side. She kicked one wheel then the other.

'Hello, anyone going to tell me what's going on?' Ed said. It would have been easier to assert himself if he wasn't staring into Lola's chest. He tried to turn his head, but the impulses that helped his neck move had stopped working. Lola stepped back a little and crouched down in front of the chair. 'Your access has been denied,' she said.

'I'm fully aware of that, thank you; obviously a malfunction with the tablet.'

'I'm afraid not, Sir,' Lola said. 'You've been reassessed, and you're…'

'Yes, yes, I know, I'm a Bernard 451 Yellow. This fact has been established. So where do I get these vouchers I'm entitled to, and how do I get into my apartment? Releasing the chair would be a start.'

'Ah, the vouchers,' Quentin said. 'Sorry about that. The vouchers are only for the first three days after assessment. They should have issued them at the validation centre.'

'No vouchers?'

'No vouchers, Sir, 'Lola said. 'You are no longer eligible.'

Ed was getting hotter. He took a breath, and tried to tell himself there was no point getting angry; there must be some mistake. 'OK, no vouchers, but can you get me into my apartment?'

'Your apartment has been cleared, Sir,' Lola said. She straightened up to her full height, and Ed found that he was staring into her blouson jacket again.

'My cat – what about Eric, what have you done with him?'

Lola looked offended. 'We're not inhuman, Sir; the cat has been rehomed.'

'What about me? Where do I get rehomed? And why can't I take Eric with me?'

'The problem is, Sir, that you have been regraded.'

Ed suppressed the urge to shout *For fuck's sake*. Instead, he said, as slowly and carefully as he could manage, 'This I know. I went to the validation centre last week. They do this once a year. There's never any change. I get a digital stamp on my tablet, my money goes in the next Wednesday as usual, and everything's as…' he gestured towards his legs, 'hunky dory as it can be.'

Lola arched her back, straightened, and crouched down again, her face so close that Ed could smell garlic on her breath. 'Unfortunately, Sir, the goal posts have been moved vis-à-vis validity.'

'No one told me.' He raised his voice.

'Best not to, Sir; it only causes alarm.'

'Well, I'm fucking alarmed now.'

Lola flinched in synch with the F word. She closed her eyelids, and then opened them slowly. 'The difficulty we have, Sir, is that you are now a Bernard 451 Yellow.'

'I don't care if I'm fucking canary yellow, can you please restore my tablet and release my chair?'

Quentin moved behind the chair, his hands on Ed's shoulders. 'Sorry mate, no can do.'

'I can appeal. I want to appeal.' His voice was getting squeakier. 'Take me to the validation centre. They'll know what to do.'

'It's a question of resources, Sir,' Lola said. 'The authorities have their budgets. We all have to live within our budgets, Sir.'

'Nothing personal, mate,' Quentin said. 'It won't take long. This will help. Lola?' He pressed down on Ed's shoulders while Lola pulled something that looked like a pen from one of the zips on her jacket.

'No! No! What the fuck…'

Lola inserted the pen into his impulse port. 'You'll be nice and relaxed. Just like having a large shot of whiskey.' His head lolled, his hands stiffened. 'I understand it can be quite pleasurable.' The sides of the chair closed in, tighter and tighter. He could hear the crack of his bones, yet felt no pain. *Just like the way they crush a car*, he thought, as if he were observing the process rather than a part of it.

As the back of Lola's vehicle opened, he saw them, stacked, wheels and backs and bones and limbs. He could make out a flattened ear in the spaces between the spokes of a wheel. He viewed it all with interest: how small the cubes of bodies and chairs, chairs and bodies, parts of one another, how beautiful.

Acknowledgements

Some of the pieces in this book have been published in *strange fruits*, and *As Long as it Takes* by Maria C. McCarthy (Cultured Llama, 2011 and 2014); in the anthologies *I Wouldn't Start From Here* (The Wild Geese Press, 2019) and *Skeins* (Linen Press 2024); in print journals *The Frogmore Papers* and *Confluence*; and on the websites *Save As Writers, Tales of the Decongested, East of the Web, Writers' Hub* and *Ink, Sweat and Tears*. Versions of 'Club Outing' and 'Flowerpot' were first published in the pamphlet *Learning to be English*, Maria C. McCarthy, 2006.

'Story' gained second place in Canterbury Festival Poet of the Year 2010. 'Cold Salt Water' and 'A Tea Party' won the Save As Writers Prose Awards in 2009 and 2011 respectively. 'More Katharine than Audrey' was the winner of the Society of Authors' Tom-Gallon Trust Award 2015.

Love and thanks to my husband Bob, and to all who support me in my writing. Particular thanks to John O'Donoghue, who came up with idea of 'The Portable McCarthy', which became this book.

Thanks also to Maggie Drury for her cover image, to Mark Holihan for cover design, and to Simon Barrow of Siglum Publishing for taking a chance on this book.

Spelling of names may not be consistent, particularly in regard to my aunts and uncles. I variously knew my Uncle Dick as Dickie or Dicky; Auntie Bridget as Brigid; Cousin Gus as Guss. My mother, I had always known as Mary Catherine; her birth certificate has her as Mary Kate; her marriage certificate as Mary Catherine.

References and Reading

'More Katharine than Audrey' was inspired by 'Life Sentence', a report by Angus Stickler, *Today*, BBC Radio 4, 28 July 2008 http://news.bbc.co.uk/today/hi/today/newsid_7523000/7523680.stm

Across the Water, Irish Women's Lives In Britain, M. Lennon, M. McAdam, J, O'Brien (Virago 1988)

An Unconsidered People: the Irish in London, Catherine Dunne (New Island, 2003)

Black Shamrocks: Accommodation Available – No Blacks, No Dogs, No Irish, Gus Michael Nwanokwu's (2016)

www.ingramcontent.com/pod-product-compliance
Ingram Content Group UK Ltd.
Pitfield, Milton Keynes, MK11 3LW, UK
UKHW041819120525
458448UK00004B/8

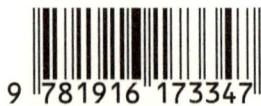